Introducing
English Pronunciation

Ship or Sheep ?

Ann Baker

CAMBRIDGE
UNIVERSITY PRESS

PUBLISHED BY THE PRESS SYNDICATE OF THE UNIVERSITY OF CAMBRIDGE
The Pitt Building, Trumpington Street, Cambridge, United Kingdom

CAMBRIDGE UNIVERSITY PRESS
The Edinburgh Building, Cambridge CB2 2RU, UK
40 West 20th Street, New York, NY 10011–4211, USA
477 Williamstown Road, Port Melbourne, VIC 3207, Australia
Ruiz de Alarcón 13, 28014 Madrid, Spain
Dock House, The Waterfront, Cape Town 8001, South Africa

http://www.cambridge.org

First published 1982
Twenty-first printing 2004

Printed in the United Kingdom at the University Press, Cambridge

A catalogue record for this book is available from the British Library

ISBN 0 521 28580 1 Teacher's guide to 'Tree or Three?' and 'Ship or Sheep?'
ISBN 0 521 28293 4 Tree or Three? Student's Book
ISBN 0 521 26355 7 Tree or Three? Set of 2 cassettes
ISBN 0 521 28354 X Ship or Sheep? Student's Book
ISBN 0 521 26358 1 Ship or Sheep? Set of 3 cassettes

Contents

Acknowledgements

I would like to thank :
Sally Mellersh of Hammersmith and West London College for compiling
the list of likely errors ; Professor J. D. O'Connor of University College,
London and Claude Boisson of Université Lyon for advice when planning
the order of presentation of sounds in *Tree or Three ?* ; Ralph Stanfield for
advice on the student difficulties sections of the teacher's notes ; Jean Crocker
and John Lipscomb for valuable discussions on *Ship or Sheep ?* ; Philippa
Lipscomb for helping with class try-outs, and Amir Pirouzan for his advice
and encouragement.

Teaching pronunciation in the early stages of EFL/ESL learning

Beginning pronunciation teaching from the beginning

Often advanced students find that they can improve all aspects of their proficiency in English except their pronunciation, and mistakes which have been repeated for years are impossible to eradicate. The long-term answer to this problem of the 'fossilised accent' is to begin teaching pronunciation from the first week of a beginners' course, and to give students so much help in the early stages that pronunciation mistakes are not learned by repetition as they otherwise inevitably are. In course planning often little or no time is allocated to pronunciation teaching at beginner level, but more time is allotted as courses progress. This process should in fact be reversed with considerably more time being allocated to pronunciation teaching at beginner than at later levels. Better a railing at the top of the cliff than a hospital at the bottom!

Selecting material appropriate to the students

Students of different mother tongues have different pronunciation problems. Particularly at beginner level, some students may be happy to spend some time on sounds which are easy for them, deriving some encouragement in the relief of finding an English sound which they *can* pronounce. But time is usually precious and if some of it is to be spent in this way, teachers must be aware of how relevant this practice is to the students' real pronunciation needs. The list of likely errors on page 138 of the Teacher's Book gives information on the difficulties of different language groups. In each unit of the Teacher's Book the *Student difficulties* section gives information on which language groups will have difficulty with that particular unit, and this can give teachers some indication of how relevant each unit is to the students. The diagnostic tests on page 134 can also be used to determine pronunciation difficulties of language groups which have not been included elsewhere, or to determine the errors of individual students.

Providing aids to students' understanding of sound production

Particularly when beginning to learn a language, students often cannot hear unfamiliar sounds or the difference between some sounds. For this reason it is often helpful to show the students how the sounds are produced. In some cases the teacher can demonstrate by pointing to the parts of the mouth that are used. However, with large classes this is not satisfactory, and in any case the production of only a few sounds can be demonstrated successfully in this way. Many teachers would also find it both difficult and time consuming to draw suitable diagrams for their students in order to show how the sounds are produced. For these reasons, each unit of *Ship or Sheep?* begins with an illustration and notes on how to produce the sound to be practised. It must be kept in mind that these are merely teaching aids and are not intended to be scientifically exact descriptions or diagrams. In *Ship or Sheep?*, vocabulary and structures used in these notes are introduced and practised beforehand.

In *Tree or Three?* each unit begins with an illustration showing how the sound is produced. Instructions on how to produce the sound have been included only in the Teacher's Book, as it is not possible to express them in language suitable for this level of students.

Providing meaningful material

One of the main problems of finding pronunciation material for students at beginner and elementary levels is the students' limited knowledge of vocabulary and structures and the resultant meaninglessness of much pronunciation practice material produced for them. In *Tree or Three?* and *Ship or Sheep?* an attempt has been made to overcome this problem in four ways:

i) Beginners can have the advantage of an appropriately graded pronunciation course by studying the early units of *Tree or Three?* in their order of presentation.

ii) Vocabulary and structures have been appropriately limited as much as possible in the two courses. Level 1 of *Cambridge English Lexicon* and the Word List from Book 1 of *Success with English* were used as a basis for vocabulary in *Tree or Three?* and *Ship or Sheep?* respectively. Particularly in the illustrated minimal pairs other words have been included when necessary, but an attempt has been made throughout to use only simple everyday words.

iii) Students are helped to understand what they are practising by illustrations of the minimal pairs. When it is made visually obvious that there is a difference between 'ship' and 'sheep', students are better motivated to succeed in this otherwise useful but seemingly meaningless exercise.

iv) Reading material in *Ship or Sheep ?* is in dialogue form and in *Tree or Three ?* each unit contains short dialogues, pair work or other illustrated practice material. This material contains a sufficient concentration of the sound to be practised without including tongue twisters or nonsense. Work on pronunciation calls for extended practice, and students are more highly motivated to listen to, repeat and even learn dialogues or other contextualised practice material than they are to practise isolated sentences which have a very high concentration of the sound to be practised, but which they are never likely to use in everyday conversation.

Linking up pronunciation teaching with other course work

Teachers very often find that students can master a pronunciation problem in 'pronunciation lessons' but inevitably lapse in general class work. The answer to this problem is not to abandon pronunciation teaching as such but to link it up with general language teaching as much as possible. For example, if students have difficulty with the sound ʃ this can be practised in lessons on :

a) describing actions using 'she' (she's reading)
b) talking about nationality (What nationality is Miss X ? Is she English ?)
c) asking for advice (What shall/should I write ?).

Ideally students should find it difficult to say whether a particular lesson is a 'pronunciation' or a 'course work' lesson. It is important to realise that few pronunciation difficulties will be overcome with one isolated 'pronunciation lesson', and to be prepared for a very slow process in which the problem is approached in as many different contexts, on as many different occasions, using as many different materials – even as many different teachers – as possible. Particularly in multi-lingual classes, students may be separated into language groups with a specialist teacher for pronunciation lessons, and this is extremely useful. But liaison is also necessary so that class teachers can continue pronunciation practice through other course work.

In this book suggestions are provided for linking up the pronunciation teaching of each unit with other course work under the headings : *Linking up with other course work* and *Further practice*. Only a few suggestions are made in each unit, and obviously these will not always fit in with every course plan. They are merely sample links, and teachers should look for other opportunities to link up their own general course work with pronunciation teaching.

Linking up pronunciation teaching and spelling

Students are very often puzzled by English spelling, and it seems to them to be not only arbitrary but unrelated to any other part of their course. Linking spelling and pronunciation provides a systematic approach to the teaching of spelling which is needed, particularly at beginner level. It also provides an opportunity for further practice and review of pronunciation material. Each unit of the teacher's notes for *Tree or Three?* includes material for this link, using vocabulary at Level 1 of *Cambridge English Lexicon*. Teachers using *Ship or Sheep?* may wish to add items appropriate to their students' level. This linking up of pronunciation and spelling should be left until after the completion of each unit and introduced in a later lesson. In *initial* practice of a new sound very often the spelling of words distracts students from the correct pronunciation rather than helping them. For this reason the minimal pairs material has been designed so that the words can be covered and initial practice done with the pictures only. Students should cut out the mask outlined at the back of their book for this purpose.

Teaching aspects of pronunciation other than sounds

Last but not least, it is essential to remember that a student who can pronounce and recognise every English sound may still be unintelligible and unable to understand the spoken language if he has not mastered English stress and intonation patterns. These are important factors in the skill of communication in English, and in almost every unit of *Tree or Three?* and *Ship or Sheep?* some aspect of stress and/or intonation is introduced and practised. Particular attention is given to word stress patterns in *Tree or Three?* and, in answer to teachers' requests, each unit of the teachers' notes for *Ship or Sheep?* provides material for word stress practice, usually in the form of a recognition test.

Practice in weak forms should also begin as early as possible, and in *Tree or Three?* three units on the sound ə provide material on this. In both books the symbol ə has been used in these units as there are so many spellings for this particular sound that a symbol helps to make students more aware of its existence. The transcription system followed is the one adopted by the *Advanced Learner's Dictionary of Current English,* and the *Longman Dictionary of Contemporary English.*

Detailed teacher's notes on
Tree or Three? **and** *Ship or Sheep?*

Level and aims of the two courses

Level

Tree or Three? Beginner to elementary.
Ship or Sheep? Lower intermediate to intermediate.

Aims

These courses are written to help students study and practise pronunciation meaningfully at an early stage by providing material which
a)   is appropriate to the students' level of English,
b)   is as communicatively valuable as possible,
c)   can be linked up with other course work.
The Teacher's Book aims to provide teachers with
a)   the means of selecting material relevant to their particular students' pronunciation needs, i.e. information on the likely difficulties of students of different mother tongues and material for testing students of mother tongues not included in this information,
b)   suggestions for lesson procedures, further practice and linking up the material with other course work.

Tree or Three ?

Design of the Student's Book

As this course is designed specifically for students at beginner or near-beginner levels, its general plan departs from the more usual order of presenting pronunciation material. In planning this course the following criteria were used in deciding the order of presentation :
a)   The more language groups having difficulty with a sound, the earlier this sound is presented in the course.
b)   The higher frequency with which a sound occurs in the beginner – early elementary vocabulary range, the earlier this sound is presented in the course. (Items from Level 1 of *Cambridge English Lexicon* were used to establish this.)
c)   Sounds which have a low frequency in this vocabulary range but which

occur in words used frequently are also presented earlier in the course. For example, there are few vocabulary items containing the sounds ð or z, but these occur in frequently used words like *the*, *this*, *they* and in the plurals of nouns and the third person singular of verbs.

Ultimately the order of presentation of the sounds has been based on subjective permutations of these three criteria. But an ordering of pronunciation material in this way makes possible a course which provides in the initial stages material which is structurally graded for beginner and early elementary students and which is also relevant to the pronunciation needs of all students. Obviously teachers may choose to teach much of the material from this course in a different order, but it is suggested that for beginners or near-beginners, the earlier units be taught in their order of presentation.

Teachers' material for each unit

This is usually divided under the following headings :

Sound production

Instructions on how to produce the sound being practised have not been included in the Student's Book. Teachers of single language classes may be able to present this information in the students' mother tongue, if this is felt to be helpful.

Student difficulties

In this section brief notes are given on the difficulties students of different mother tongues are likely to encounter in each unit. Speakers of the following languages are mentioned where relevant : Arabic, Chinese, Dutch, French, Farsi (spoken by Afghans and Iranians), Finnish, German, Greek, Gujerati, Hebrew, Hungarian, Italian, Japanese, Portuguese, Punjabi, Scandinavian languages (Swedish, Norwegian, Danish), Serbo-Croat, Slavic languages (Russian, Polish, Czech), Spanish, Turkish, Urdu, Indo-Chinese languages (Vietnamese, Lao, Thai, Khmer). Where difficulties of Lao speakers are mentioned, this information applies equally to speakers of Thai.

These notes are extremely brief, and for more detail teachers may find it useful to refer to the two series of publications *Asian Language Notes* and *English a New Language* prepared by the Language Teaching Branch of the Commonwealth Department of Education (P.O. Box 826, Woden, A.C.T., 2606, Australia).

Linking up with course work

In this section some specific suggestions are made for linking up the material in the unit with other course work. In some units the link is made with teaching a specific structure, for example, Unit 14 ŋ with teaching the Present Continuous tense. In other units the link is more functional, for example, Unit 40 j with teaching formal introductions.

A summary of language items is listed on pages 8 and 9 to assist teachers and course planners in drawing up a teaching programme which links up this material with other course work.

Suggested procedures

This section contains information on specific language items and suggested procedures for teaching each exercise. Teaching procedures are outlined particularly for less experienced teachers, and it is expected that procedures used will vary according to the students' level and the teachers' own methods.

MINIMAL PAIR EXERCISES

Procedures for teaching these are outlined on page 104 (steps 2–3).

The minimal pair sentences can be used to give a sound recognition test, and these have been recorded as a test on the cassette, with answers on page 120 of the Student's Book.

Further examples of minimal pair words are given in this section of the Teacher's Book. Often pair words within the beginner–elementary vocabulary range do not exist. Teachers should decide whether or not to use these further examples depending on the students' level and need for further practice, and the teachers' ability to illustrate, explain or translate the words given.

Further practice

This section provides teaching material for further practice if this is needed. In some units this section gives a different link with course work and teachers may wish to use this material in another lesson.

Spelling

It is suggested that this material be introduced after teaching each unit as this provides a review of words taught in the unit. In earlier units the examples given for each spelling of the sound are divided under subheadings **B** (Beginner) and **E** (Elementary) so that teachers can introduce a shorter list of examples to Beginners.

The simplest way of introducing this material is to ask students, for example, 'How do you write/spell the sound ɪː?' and build up a blackboard summary of lists of words for each spelling of the sound, using students' suggestions whenever possible.

Pronunciation of some words

This section is included particularly for teachers whose mother tongue is not English, but native speakers may also find it useful to refer to.

Summary of language items in each unit

1	s	What's this? It's a ship. They're ships.
2	z	Is this a horse? No, it isn't. These are flowers and those are trees.
3	ə	Are these plates? No, they aren't.
4	θ	Ordinal numbers 1–10. Which horse is third?
5	ð	Which boy is in the first picture? The boy (one) with the book.
6	iː	Ordering food in a restaurant. A cheese sandwich, please.
7	ɪ	Adjectives: It's a big ship. Stress contrasts in numbers from 13–30 to 19–90.
		Noun plurals ending in 'es'.
		This is a box. These are boxes.
8	f	Prepositions: on, in front of.
9	v	Have they got a television? No, they haven't.
10	w	Talking about the weather.
		Times: quarter / twenty past.
11	ə	A cup of coffee / bowl of fruit.
		Have you got the time? Yes, it's one o'clock.
		Have you got a telephone? Yes, I have.
12	m	Come to the market with me.
13	n	Times of day: a.m. / p.m.; in the morning / afternoon / evening.
14	ŋ	Present Continuous tense: What are you doing?
		What's Ben doing? What are the children doing?
15	e	Jenny is better than Ben. Fred is the best student.
16	æ	They are all very happy except for Jack.
17	ʌ	Family relationships.
		Patsy Young is Dan Monday's mother.
18	ɑː	Can you see me? Yes, I can / No, I can't.
		Are the glasses on the table? Yes, they are / No, they aren't.
19	h	Whose hat is this? It's his / hers.
		Hello. How are you? I'm fine. / All right.

20	ɒ	Requests in a shop:
		I want a . . . / Have you got any . . .
21	ɔː	Adjectives: large / small; long / short: tall / short.
		A long wall with a small door in it.
22	ə	Can you hear? Yes, I can.
23	ɜː	Simple Present tense in describing daily routine:
		She walks to work.
24	l	Adjectives:
		That hotel is full. Those hotels are all full.
25	r	Who's throwing a ball along the street?
26	silent r	What a large fork!
		I don't understand the word 'north'.
27	r/silent r	Possessive pronouns: her, your, our, their.
28	ɪə/eə	Asking for directions: Excuse me. Where's the airport?
		There's a newspaper on the table.
		My newspaper isn't there.
29	ʊ	Don't push it! Pull it!
30	uː	Do you like music? Yes, I do.
31	t	What a fat cat! What fat cats!
32	d	Do you like hard beds? Yes, I do. Do you?
33	aʊ	How many cows are there?
34	əʊ	Where are you going?
35	s/linking s	Do you like this seat? Whose seat is it? Who's sleeping?
36	ʃ	Is she Scottish or English?
37	ʒ	She usually wakes up at seven o'clock.
38	tʃ	There's a watch / some cheese on the table.
		How much cheese is there? There's enough / too much / too
		little . . .
39	dʒ	Which fridge is the cheese in?
40	j	I like your glasses. Thank you.
41	eɪ	What's the baby playing with?
42	ɔɪ	These are noisy boys.
43	aɪ	I like / don't like climbing.
44	p/b	What's his job?
45	k/g	Be careful! Carry the cups carefully.
		Mr Green likes dogs.
46	s/z	Which man makes clocks?

Unit 1   s (sun)

Note: Other units on s: Unit 35 (s/linking s), Unit 46 (s/z in final consonant clusters).

Sound production

Touch your side teeth with the sides of your tongue. Put your tongue forward. Do not use your voice.

Student difficulties

Most students can pronounce s. Many students have considerable difficulty with consonant clusters containing this sound.

s + *consonant clusters*
Example: *spoon* may be pronounced by speakers of the following languages: German ʃpu:n; Farsi, Arabic, Turkish, Spanish espu:n or ɪspu:n; Portuguese əʃpu:n; Vietnamese bu:n; some other Asian languages pu:n or sɪpu:n.

consonant + s *clusters*
Example: *cats* may be pronounced by speakers of the following languages: Chinese, Spanish, Indo-Chinese kæt; Italian kætsə; Arabic, Turkish, some Asian languages kætɪs.

Linking up with course work

Structures in this unit are usually introduced very early in most beginner's courses:
Exercise 1 What's this? It's a pencil.
Exercise 2 What's this? A bus? Yes/No.
Exercise 3 They're cups.
For complete beginners postpone the teaching of Exercise 3 until plurals have been introduced in general structure teaching.

Suggested procedures

EXERCISE I

Note: Weak form of 'a': ə.
    For complete beginners and/or students with particular difficulty the following can be introduced separately: items 1–5 (medial or final s); items 6–12 (s in consonant clusters).
    Flashcards made from the pictures in this exercise can be used again in Units 2–5.

Steps
1 Students repeat the words looking at the pictures in the book or
flashcards: bus, a bus, etc. If necessary practise clusters with the aid of a
blackboard build up of sounds, for example:
sssss   sssssspoon   spoon
desssss   dessssk   desk
2 Check pronunciation of 'it's', which is very difficult for some students.
Use forward and back chaining with aid of blackboard:
it   it's;   s   ts   it's.
3 Example:
Teacher: Picture 1 (or flashcard) What's this?
Student(s): It's a bus.
4 Check pronunciation of 'What's this?' wɒts ðɪs as in step 2. This is very
difficult for many students, and it is wise to ignore mispronunciation of ð
here.
5 Pair work as in the Example using book or flashcards.

EXERCISE 2

Note: Linking of s sounds in: Miss Smith; What's this, Sam? This is practised
again in Unit 35.
Falling intonation in 'wh' question: What's this? Rising intonation in
Yes/No question: A bus? (Is it a bus?)

Steps
1 Introduce the characters in the dialogue with the illustration: It's a teacher.
It's Miss Smith. Miss Smith is a teacher. It's Sam. It's a student. Sam is a
student.
2 Students listen to the dialogue on tape or read by the teacher.
3 Blackboard practice for joining s sounds:
MissssSmith   Miss Smith   Miss Smith   What's thissssssSam?   What's
this Sam?   What's this, Sam?
4 Repetition of dialogue with role playing; pair practice.

EXERCISE 3

Note: The letter 's' for plural is usually pronounced z but following the
sounds t/p/k/f/θ it is pronounced s.
Final consonant clusters in Example and items 1–2: ps; items 3–5: ts;
items 6–8: ks. It may be helpful to divide the teaching of this exercise in this
way as these consonant clusters are difficult. Note particularly item 8, desks.
Flashcards made for this exercise can be used again in Units 2–5. It is useful
to have the singular picture on the front and the plural on the back of the
card.

Steps
1 Students look at the book or flashcards and listen to the sentences read by the teacher or on tape.
2 The following blackboard practice may help students who have difficulty in making these final consonants relatively quiet sounds.
CUp   CUpS
SHIp   SHIpS
SHOp   SHOpS
3 Students practise sentences from the book or with flashcards.

EXERCISE 4

Review of word stress in Unit 1. Introduction to symbols used for stress patterns.

Further practice

consonant + s *clusters*
taxi, six, sixteen, sixty
ts   boats, skirts, coats, shirts, streets, lights
ps   shapes, tops, stamps
ks   backs, clocks, socks, sticks, trucks

s *+ consonant clusters*
stamp, street, sister, school, skirt, square, sky; a small smile; a slow snail; a sleeping policeman

s *sounds*
Yes, sir; house seventeen; class seven; horse six; a bus stop; six spoons; a nice smile

Spelling

The sound s is usually written with the letter 's'.
Examples: sit, sun, sister, desk, stop, bus

Other spellings: ($\boxed{B}$ = Beginner; $\boxed{E}$ = Elementary)
ss $\boxed{B}$ class, lesson, Miss; $\boxed{E}$ dress, grass, across, address
se $\boxed{B}$ horse, house; $\boxed{E}$ worse
c $\boxed{B}$ bicycle, exercise; $\boxed{E}$ cinema, ceiling
ce $\boxed{B}$ policeman, face; $\boxed{E}$ dance, nice, office, once, pence, place
x   (pronounced ks) $\boxed{B}$ six, box, taxi, exercise; $\boxed{E}$ next

Pronunciation of some words in this unit

bicycle	baɪsɪkl	**stu**dent	stjuːdnt
po**lice**man	pəliːsmən	**di**alogue	daɪəlɒg
pencil	pensl	**e**xercise	eksəsaɪz
answer	ɑːnsə	**u**nit	juːnɪt
listen	lɪsn	e**xam**ple	ɪgzɑːmpl
picture	pɪktʃə	re**peat**	rɪpiːt

Unit 2   z (zoo)

Note: Other units on z: Unit 46 (s/z in final consonant clusters). Further practice of z in final consonant clusters is also included in Unit 24 Exercise 3, Unit 32 Exercise 2, Unit 45 Exercise 4.

Sound production

First practise the sound s. Show students that the voice is used when making the sound z but not s. Demonstrate by placing your hand on your throat; show vibration with your hand when saying z.

Student difficulties

Many students have difficulty with this sound, particularly speakers of German, Italian, Portuguese, Spanish, Turkish, Scandinavian and Asian languages. The most common error is to confuse this sound with s, particularly at the end of a word, although Spanish speakers have difficulty in all positions. Japanese speakers may confuse it with dz, and speakers of some other Asian languages may confuse it with dʒ.

Linking up with course work:

EXERCISE 2

Is this a box? No, it isn't. / Yes, it is.

EXERCISE 3

These are flowers and those are trees. For complete beginners Exercise 3 can be postponed until after introducing plurals and *these/those*. If introducing *these/those* through this exercise, begin with demonstration. For example: (standing near tables and pointing), 'These are tables and those are windows'; (standing near windows), 'These are windows and those are tables.' Practise with other realia before beginning the exercise.

Suggested procedures

EXERCISE 1

For suggested teaching procedures for minimal pairs, see page 104. Contrasts for further practice: said/z; piece/peas; price/prize; ass/as.

EXERCISE 2

Note: Rising intonation in Yes/No questions.
   Pronunciation of isn't: ɪznt.

Steps
1 Students look at cartoon and listen to the sentences on tape or read by the teacher. Ask: 'Is it a house or a box?'
2 Students listen and repeat sentences from the cartoon.
3 Dramatisation of the cartoon. Sketch the two 'paintings' on the blackboard, bring a student to the front and ask of the first 'painting', 'Is it a box?' etc. Thought words in the last frame can be said in a whisper aside to the rest of the class. Two students perform this.
4 Pair work as in the Example.

Extension: Use flashcards from Unit 1 Exercise 1 for pair practice. Example:
Picture 1   *Teacher*:   bicycle
            Student A: Is this a bicycle?
            Student B: No, it isn't. It's a bus.

EXERCISE 3

Note: Except where words end in the sounds t/p/k/f/θ the letter 's' for plural is always pronounced z, so it is important that students can make this sound at the end of a word.
   Weak forms: and ənd; are ə.
   Pronunciation of final letter 'r' before a vowel in frame 6: Those are aeroplanes.

Steps
1 Practise the words in each frame first before beginning sentences. Words ending in consonant clusters: girls, bicycles, aeroplanes, dogs, birds. Use back chaining for these.
2 For complete beginners start with first half of sentence only: These are flowers.   These are boys, etc.

Extension
a)   Use plural side of flashcards from Unit 1 Exercise 3. Stand a row of students holding cards on either side of the room. The first student in each row shows his card and makes an appropriate sentence, for example: (showing 'cats') 'These are cats and those are ...' etc. Also

students from the body of the class make sentences appropriate to their proximity to the two pictures being shown.

b)   Use flashcards from Unit 1 Exercise 3 to practise, for example: Picture 1

    Teacher: shops

    Student A: Are these (those) shops?

    Student B: No, they aren't.

Note: Weak form of 'are' ə in the question. See next Unit Exercise 3.

EXERCISE 4

Review of word stress in Units 1 and 2. Preparation for Exercise 1 in the next unit where some letters of these words will be printed with phonetic spelling to show pronunciation of the sound ə.

Further practice

Final z in plurals: Word groups: families; bodies; schools; times; rooms.

Beginners: Introduce and practise one word group with picture on blackboard.

Elementary: Possible class activity: write two or more of these headings on the blackboard. Then read words from the groups at random. Students decide which group they belong to and help to make a list under the right heading on the blackboard.

families	*bodies*		*schools*

		fingers	teachers, pupils,
		hands	lessons, questions,
		arms	answers, examples,
		heads	words, numbers,
		eyes	letters, pictures,
		ears	pens, pencils

mothers, fathers,
boys, girls,
brothers, sisters
babies

legs
toes

times	*rooms*
hours, days,	chairs, tables,
years, mornings,	beds, cupboards,
afternoons,	walls, corners
evenings	

Spelling

The sound z is usually written with the letter 's'.
Examples: ($\boxed{\text{B}}$ = Beginner; $\boxed{\text{E}}$ = Elementary) $\boxed{\text{B}}$ is, isn't, trees, birds; $\boxed{\text{E}}$
as, does, has, his, easy, husband, music, present, visit, trousers

Plurals: See examples in Exercise 3 and word groups for further practice.
Other words: $\boxed{\text{E}}$ spoons, stars, balls, bags, friends; $\boxed{\text{E}}$ stories, taxis, colours,
doctors, rivers, stairs, animals, hills, hotels, meals, eggs, roads, towns, trains,
farms

Other spellings:
z/ze   zoo, size
se $\boxed{\text{B}}$ please, these, those, exercise, nose; $\boxed{\text{E}}$ because, whose, noise, lose
x   (pronounced gz) example

Pronunciation of some words in this unit

Sue su:	**isn't** ɪznt
buzz bʌz	**flow**ers flaʊəz
zoo zu:	**aero**planes eərəpleɪnz
pence pens	

Unit 3   ə (a camera)

Note: Other units on ə: 11, 22.

Sound production and student difficulties

ə is close to the English sound ɜ: but it is very short. All students seem to
have difficulty, although ə (the shwa) may not be a difficult sound for them
to pronounce. The difficulty for intermediate and advanced students seems
to lie in:
a)   simply not having been taught to use it from the beginning – and then,
     having not used it with such great frequency as this sound occurs, it is
     difficult for them to change;
b)   the lack of any prop from spelling to show where it can be used;
c)   the fact that students can get away with not using it: although they may
     not always understand, they will always be understood;
d)   lack of awareness of how stress can change this sound.
The shwa is used a lot in weak forms of very common words, and one
problem in teaching it is that it disappears when these words are considered
in isolation. For example, the words 'have' and 'are' are pronounced hæv
and ɑ: in isolation, but in running speech most native speakers would say

həv and ə in sentences like: 'Have you got a watch?' 'Who are they?'
Students may never manage to speak like this, but at least by being
introduced to the shwa at an early stage they will have less difficulty in
understanding spoken English.

The symbol ə is used in the units on ə as the normal spellings do not help to
make students aware of this sound. Only words which have already been
taught with normal spelling are introduced in these units. During these
lessons students should practise from the words written on the blackboard
with normal spelling as well.

Linking up with course work

Exercise 1: weak form of the indefinite articles *a, an.*

Exercise 2: weak form of *are* and *and.*

Exercise 3: weak form of *are* in questions, for example: 'Are these plates?'.

Strong form of *are* in short answers, for example: 'Yes, they are. / No,
they aren't'.

Link up with practice of asking questions about nationality/job/marital
status, for example: 'Are you English/an engineer/married?'

If these weak forms are used constantly in general course teaching, this
unit should merely consolidate for students what they have already
practised.

Suggested procedures

EXERCISE I

Note: Different letters can make the sound ə, here: o, a, er.
    ə is never in the stressed part of the word or sentence.

Steps
1 Students look at and repeat the words from Unit 2 Exercise 4 to remind
   them of the normal spelling of these words.
2 Students look at and repeat words in the word list at the beginning of this
   exercise.
3 Teacher or students write normal spelling of these words on the
   blackboard. If possible discuss the note on different spellings for ə (above).
4 Demonstrate stress patterns of these words, for example, by tapping with
   a ruler. Students do this too while repeating the words again. If possible
   discuss the note on ə and stress (above).
5 Use the method in step 4 to practise items 1–5 and sentences as in the
   Example.

Extension: Practise again with flashcards from Unit 1 Exercise 1 and singular
pictures from Exercise 3, paying particular attention to the sound ə in 'a'.

EXERCISE 2

Note: Weak forms of *are* in the question.
Strong form in both answers.

Steps
1 Students repeat the sample question and answer and read the question with normal spelling from the blackboard. Also on the blackboard show stress on *are* in the answers: 'Yes, they are. / No they aren't.
2 Pair practice.
3 Students write a sentence using the symbol ə.

Extension: Use the pictures in this exercise or flashcards of plural pictures from Unit 1 Exercise 3 to practise: 'What are these?' with weak form of *are*. On blackboard show contrast of falling intonation in this question with rising intonation in: 'Are these plates?'

Further practice

Students begin a vocabulary list of words that have or can have this sound. (See spelling lists below.) If students already have their own vocabulary list or notebook for other lessons, review this and make the symbol ə where this sound occurs. If possible use the symbol for words which are always pronounced with this sound and (ə) for words which can sometimes have this sound, for example: are.

Students can repeat Unit 2 Exercise 3 with particular attention to the weak forms of *are* and *and*.

Spelling

The sound ə is usually written with the letters a, o, e or er.

(ə) *words which can have this sound in a sentence (weak forms)*:
a   am, a, an, and, as, at, shall
o   for, from, of, to
e   the

ə *words which always have this sound*: (**B** = Beginner; **E** = Elementary)
a   **B** again, policeman, woman; **E** about, across, address, another, cinema, husband, camera
o   **B** aeroplane, o'clock, policeman, today; **E** forget, second, tonight
e   **B** hello, open, policeman; **E** cinema, quiet, camera
er   **B** afternoon, answer, brother, exercise, father, flower, letter, mother, number, paper, sister, teacher, understand, water **E** after, another, better, corner, finger, matter, never, other, over, quarter, remember, river, summer, supper, trousers, under, weather, winter, yesterday.

Other spellings:

[B] colour kʌlə	picture pɪktʃə
question kwestʃən	
[E] doctor dɒktə	autumn ɔ:təm
visitor vɪzɪtə	tired taɪəd
animal ænəml	fire faɪə

Pronunciation of some words in this unit

question kwestʃən	**di**alogue daɪəlɒg
answer ɑ:nsə	**aero**plane eərəpleɪn
flower flaʊə	po**lice**man pəli:smən
exercise eksəsaɪz	

Unit 4   θ (thin)

Sound production

Put the tip of your tongue between your teeth, touching your top teeth. Blow out air between your top teeth and your tongue. Do not use your voice. This is a quiet sound.

Student difficulties

Nearly all except Greek and Spanish students have great difficulty with this sound, confusing it with s or t. There are few suitable words at this level for minimal pair work and generally the sound θ has a low frequency in the beginner's vocabulary range.

   Showing students the tongue position is very helpful in teaching this sound. It is important to give students a physical demonstration of how to make the sound, saying, for example: 'This is my mouth. This is my tongue. These are my teeth. Put your tongue between your teeth.' Draw a large coloured blackboard sketch of the tongue position, and spend enough time practising the sound in isolation before beginning the exercises. At this stage providing students with a sustained model of the sound (i.e. pronouncing it without stopping for about 5–10 seconds) helps them to distinguish it from t. Knowing that the sound they are aiming at is a very *quiet* sound also seems to help students.

Linking up with course work

EXERCISE 2

Ordinal numbers 1–10 (first, second, etc.) Students should have learnt the cardinal numbers 1–10 before this unit. They may already be familiar with some ordinal numbers through the teacher's class instructions: 'Look at the first picture' etc. If students have only heard: 'Look at picture number one' etc., and particularly if the situation used in Exercise 2 (a horse race) is culturally unfamiliar to them, precede this unit with some use of ordinal numbers in general class instructions.

Suggested procedures

EXERCISE 1

For suggested teaching procedures for minimal pairs, see page 104.
Contrasts for further practice:
s/θ sing/thing; sink/think; moss/moth
t/θ tree/three; tin/thin; boat/both; true/through

EXERCISE 2

Note: Abbreviations for ordinal numbers.
Steps
1 Students repeat ordinal numbers.
2 See suggestions for linking up with course work (above). If horse racing is completely unknown to students begin with a situation familiar to them, for example, a national sports competition or a blackboard sketch of children running a race.
3 Horses have funny names. What's the fifth horse's name? Which horse is ninth? etc.
4 Students practise the question: Which horse is first? etc.
5 Practise as in the Example.

Extension: Use the current page of a calendar to practise numbers with dates.

Further practice

B Use familiar place names to practise: 'Is it north or south of here?'
E 'What's the opposite of: north (south); thick (thin); something (nothing)?'

Spelling

The sound θ is always written with the letters 'th'.
Examples: (B = beginners; E = Elementary) B mouth, month, thirsty, three, thirteen, thirty; E both, north, south, nothing, thick, thin, through, throw, think

Pronunciation of some words in this unit

mouth	maʊθ	eighth	eɪtθ
thumb	θʌm	**su**nny	sʌnɪ
second	sekənd	**Mickey**	mɪkɪ
fifth	fɪfθ	**Sammy**	sæmɪ
seventh	sevnθ	**Bir**die	bɜːdɪ

Unit 5 ð (feather)

Sound production

First practise the sound θ. Use your voice to make ð.

Student difficulties

Nearly all except Greek and Spanish students have great difficulty with this sound, confusing it with z or d. There are no suitable words at this level for minimal pair work on these contrasts, but as with the sound θ, showing students the tongue position is very helpful. See suggestions under *Student difficulties* in Unit 4. When practising the sound in isolation, show use of the voice in ð by movement of your hand on your throat. A sustained model of this sound also helps students to distinguish it from d. Although the sound ð has a very low frequency in the beginner's vocabulary range, it occurs in some very common words like *the*, *this*, *that*, etc., and it is therefore important for students to master it at an early stage.

Linking up with course work

In most beginner's courses the indefinite article (*a*, *an*) is introduced first. In this course the definite article (*the*) is used for the first time in this unit. If students have not already met the definite article in their general course work or if they have particular difficulty with articles, it may be helpful to precede work on pictures 1–8 in Exercise 1 with the following practice:

Picture 1 That's a boy with a book.
Picture 2 That's a boy with a bicycle, etc.

Suggested procedures

EXERCISE 1

Note: Weak form of *the*: ðə or ðɪ.
   Pronunciation of *with*: Received Pronunciation (R.P.) English wɪð; some varieties of English: wɪθ.

Steps
1 Students listen and repeat words from the blackboard: *this, there, the, with*
2 Students read or repeat the initial four sentences in this exercise, listen to the text on Pictures 1 and 2, and repeat the answer: 'The boy with the book.' (Note that 'The boy with a book.' is also correct here but not 'A boy with a book.')
3 Students practise the answers for pictures 2–8.
4 Students practise the questions, for example:
Teacher: The sixth picture
Student(s): Which man is in the sixth picture?
5 Pair practice as in the example.

EXERCISE 2

This is an extension of the structures used in Exercise 1, and students should be able to practise this without any preliminary drilling.

Further practice

A quick repetition of all or some of the following exercises provides a review of Units 1–4 with practice in the sound ð:

Unit 1 Exercise 1: (flashcards or books) What's this?
Unit 1 Exercise 2: (flashcards or books) They're cups.
Unit 2 Exercise 3: These are flowers and those are trees (or use plural flashcards from Unit 1 Exercise 2 for this structure).
Unit 3 Exercise 2: Are these plates? No, they aren't (or use flashcards from Unit 1 Exercise 2).
Unit 4 Exercise 2: Example:
Teacher: What about Flower?
Student(s): That's the seventh horse.

Spelling

The sound ð is always written with the letters 'th'.
Examples: ($\boxed{\text{B}}$ = Beginners; $\boxed{\text{E}}$ = Elementary) $\boxed{\text{B}}$ brother, father, mother, that, the, there, these, they, this, those, with; $\boxed{\text{E}}$ another, other, their, them, then, weather, without

Pronunciation of some words in this unit

with	wɪð	**fa**ther	fɑːðə
mother	mʌðə	**fea**ther	feðə
brother	brʌðə		

Unit 6   i: (sheep)

Sound production

Open your mouth very little to make the sound i:. i: is a very long sound, although it is shorter before final unvoiced consonants.

Student difficulties

Most students do not have difficulty with this sound, although some students, particularly Greek and Hebrew speakers, do not make it long enough and may confuse it with ɪ. For most students, however, this unit merely introduces the sound i: for contrastive work in the next unit with ɪ, which many students find difficult.

Note on vowels: Lao speakers have a strong tendency to place a glottal stop before all vowels at the beginning of words.

Linking up with course work

EXERCISE 1

Short requests as given in a restaurant or shop, for example: 'A cheese sandwich, please.'

EXERCISE 2

Pronunciation of numbers (13–19); letters in the alphabet with the sound i:.

Suggested procedures

EXERCISE 1

Note: Pronunciation of 'coffee': R.P. English kɒfɪ, some varieties of English kɒfi:.
   Falling intonation at the end of a list in these requests.
   Weak forms: *of* əv; *a* ə; *and* ənd; *for* fə.
   Some students tend to over-stress the word 'please'.

Steps
1 Introduce the restaurant situation with the picture: These people are in a restaurant. This is the menu. Students repeat items on the menu.
2 Students listen to the requests on tape or read by the teacher, and repeat or read these.
3 Practice from the menu should come first. The class should listen to at least one role play with the teacher playing the part of the waitress. Begin by pointing to the first person in the second picture: Miss X, you are the first person. Look at the menu. A cheese sandwich? A meat sandwich? Tea? Coffee?

4 Students practise role playing in groups of 4 or 5 with one of them taking the part of the waitress and trying to remember the orders.

EXERCISE 2

Note: The first part of this exercise is preparatory to work in Unit 7 Exercise 3 where students will be practising the contrasting stress patterns of thir**teen**, **thir**ty, etc.

Some students mispronounce these letters in the alphabet even though the sound i: has no difficulty for them, and this causes confusion in oral spelling of words. Particularly the letters 'e' and 'a' are confused. Some students also pronounce the letter 'k' as ki:.

Students should practise using 'double e' and 'double o' when spelling words aloud.

Extension: If students have particular difficulty with pronouncing these letters of the alphabet, divide the class into two teams for a spelling competition with students recording scores on the blackboard. Each student takes a turn to ask a member of the other team to spell a word from this list.

Further practice

Role playing: Requests in a shop based on the following (to be written on the blackboard):

1 kilo	of	cheese	peas	, please.
3 kilos		meat	sweets	
		beans	tea	

Each customer gives 2–4 items in his request, which the shopkeeper should be able to repeat.

Spelling

The sound i: is usually written with the letters 'ee', 'ea' or 'e'.
Examples: (**B** = Beginner; **E** = Elementary)
ee   **B** thirteen, fourteen etc., green, sheep, street, three, tree; **E** between, need, see, sleep, sweet
ea   **B** please, read, tea, teacher; **E** cheap, clean, east, easy, eat, leaf, leave, meal, sea, speak
e   **B** he, she, we, these; **E** be, being, evening, me

Other spellings: **B** policeman, people; **E** ceiling, piece.

Pronunciation of some words in this unit

| menu | menju: | coffee | kɒfɪ |
| sandwiches | sænwɪdʒɪz | seventeen | sevnti:n |

Unit 7 ɪ (ship)

Sound production

First practise the sound iː. Then open your mouth a *little* more. iː is a long sound. ɪ is a short sound.

Student difficulties

This sound occurs very frequently in the beginner's vocabulary range and nearly all students have difficulty with it, confusing it with iː. Arabic speakers may also confuse it with e. When practising the two sounds iː and ɪ in isolation, knowing that ɪ is a much shorter, quieter sound than iː seems to help students. Encourage students to use a mirror to check lip position.

Linking up with course work

EXERCISE 2

Common adjectives: It's a little baby.

EXERCISE 3

Numbers: 30, 40, 50, 60, 70, 80, 90.

EXERCISE 4

Formation of noun plurals with 'es', for example: boxes. If adjectives have not yet been introduced in general course teaching, begin work on the first part of Exercise 2 with pair sketches on the blackboard of familiar objects (or using realia) to illustrate, for example: It's big. It's little. It's a big house. It's a little house/box/glass/pencil/spoon. If possible do this in a previous lesson. Note that the stress pattern in these pairs will be the same as in the second half of Exercise 2, i.e.: It's a **little box**. It's a **big box**.

Suggested procedures

EXERCISE I

For suggested teaching procedures for minimal pairs, see page 104. Contrasts for further practice: eat/it; cheap/chip; seat/sit; heel/hill.

EXERCISE 2

Note: In normal sentence stress both adjective and noun are stressed with major stress on the noun, for example: What's that? It's a **little bean**. (This pattern is used in the first part of this exercise.) But when two or more adjectives are contrasted major stress is on the adjective, for example: This is a **li**ttle **ba**by; That's a **big ba**by (This pattern is used in the second part of this exercise.)

In English if the sex of a baby is known it is referred to as 'he' or 'she', but if not known, 'it'.

Steps
1 Students listen and repeat: big, little.
2 Students complete the sentences in the first part, for example:
   Teacher: Picture 1. What's that?
   Student(s): It's a little sheep.
3 Students listen and repeat the adjectives listed below the second set of pictures. Note that some Asian students who do not have difficulty with the sound ɪ elsewhere may pronounce it iː in final position. Note that in some varieties of English final ɪ sound is pronounced iː.
4 If any of these words are new to students show meaning through the pictures. (Example: Picture 3: heavy. It's heavy. It's a heavy baby.) Check understanding. Students repeat.
5 Students make a sentence for each picture as in the Example.

EXERCISE 3

Note: Students very often confuse, for example, four**teen** fɔːtiːn and **for**ty fɔːtɪ. Particularly if there is some question about which number is said, they will stress the last syllable of forty, making the problem worse. Note that when counting – 13, 14, 15, etc. – one tends to stress the first syllable of these words more than in other contexts, and as students usually learn these numbers by counting, they then find it difficult to stress these words correctly so as to distinguish them from 30, 40, 50, etc.

Steps
1 Students read or repeat these numbers reading the columns horizontally. emphasize stress by, for example, tapping with a ruler.
2 Write the numbers for the second and third columns at random on the blackboard. Get a student to stand at the blackboard and point to the numbers you say; then other students take turns to say the numbers clearly enough for a student to point to the correct one.

EXERCISE 4

Note: This exercise provides a review of the following sounds practised in Units 1–7: s/z/ə/ð/iː/ɪ.

Words ending in the sounds s/z/ʃ/tʃ/ʒ/dʒ form the plural with ɪz in R.P. English (some varieties of English əz).

Note spelling: words ending in 'e', add 's'; others, add 'es'. Note change of pronunciation in the word itself in haʊs/haʊzɪz.

Weak forms of *a* ə and *are* ə.

Some students have difficulty with word stress, pronouncing, for xample, bɒksez instead of bɒksɪz.

'teps

Students listen and repeat plural words at the beginning of this exercise.
Emphasise stress by, for example, tapping with a ruler.
Students practise sentences as in the Example.

urther practice

'inal ɪ *sounds*: (R.P. English) Practise pronunciation of days of the week:
nʌndɪ/tju:zdɪ/wenzdɪ/θɜ:zdɪ/fraɪdɪ/sætədɪ/sʌndɪ.

Plurals ending in the sound ɪz/: dress, class, address, six, size, noise, sentence,
vatch, lunch, match, church, page, age, fridge, garage.

;pelling

The sound ɪ is usually written with the letter 'i', and with the letter'y' at the
end of a word.
Examples: ($\boxed{\text{B}}$ = Beginners; $\boxed{\text{E}}$ = Elementary)

i $\boxed{\text{B}}$ big, fifteen, finger, fish, give, hill, in, is, it, kitchen, listen, little, milk,
     morning, picture, sit, ship, sister, six, stick, this, which, window, with
     $\boxed{\text{E}}$ bit, bring, ceiling, cinema, drink, evening, finish, him, his, ill,
     important, live, middle, music, nothing, office, quick, rich, ring, river,
     spring, still, swim, taxi, thick, thin, thing, visit, will, wind, winter

y $\boxed{\text{B}}$ any, angry, baby, dirty, easy, empty, family, funny, happy, heavy,
     hungry, money, penny, thirsty, very, twenty, thirty, etc.
     $\boxed{\text{E}}$ already, badly, body, carry, copy, early, every, lorry, many, only,
     party, really, story, study

Other spellings:

e $\boxed{\text{B}}$ eleven ɪlevn; example ɪgzɑ:mpl; $\boxed{\text{E}}$ because, before, begin, behind,
     beside, between, market, pocket, remember rɪmembə, television telɪvɪʒn
u, ee $\boxed{\text{B}}$ minute mɪnɪt, coffee kɒfɪ
ay $\boxed{\text{B}}$ yesterday jestədɪ, Monday mʌndɪ, Tuesday tju:zdɪ, etc.

Pronunciation of some words in this unit

baby	beɪbɪ	**thir**ty	θɜ:tɪ
babies	beɪbɪz	**for**ty	fɔ:tɪ
heavy	hevɪ	**bo**xes	bɒksɪz
hungry	hʌngrɪ	**no**ses	nəʊzɪz
thirsty	θɜ:stɪ	**hou**ses	haʊzɪz
dirty	dɜ:tɪ		

Unit 8   f (fan)

Sound production

Touch your top teeth with your bottom lip. Blow out air between your lip and your teeth.

Student difficulties

Although most students do not have difficulty with f it is a difficult sound for speakers of Hebrew and many Asian languages with the exception of Chinese and Vietnamese. It is usually confused with the sound p. Japanese students often confuse it with h.

Linking up with course work

It is assumed here that students know the prepositions 'on' and 'in front of'.

Suggested procedures

1 Minimal pair practice for students with particular difficulty (see above):
   p/f   pence/fence; pull/full; put/foot; pork/fork; copy/coffee
   h/f   hat/fat; hill/fill; hive/five; hair/fair; honey/funny
2 Students listen and repeat the words in the illustration. Check particularly pronunciation of consonant clusters: $f+l$; $f+r$.
3 Students complete and read the five sentences.

Further practice

Students read the following groups of words from the blackboard and decide which word doesn't belong in each group:
1 wife knife father grandfather
2 fifty four fork fifteen
3 fly fish fruit food
4 office floor telephone flower
5 football foot finger face
6 funny fat careful afternoon

Spelling

The sound f is usually written with the letter 'f'.
Examples: ($\boxed{\text{B}}$ = Beginner; $\boxed{\text{E}}$ = Elementary) $\boxed{\text{B}}$ face, family, fat, father, fifteen, fifty, finger, fire, first, fish, five, floor, flower, fly, foot, fork, forty, four, fourteen, friend, front, fruit, funny, grandfather, leaf

E after, afternoon, before, careful, farm, find, finish, follow, food, football, for, forget, from, full, half, often

Other spellings:
ph   telephone
ff   off, office
fe   wife, knife

Pronunciation of some words in this unit

Fred	fred	te**le**phone	teləfəʊn
Fay	feɪ	knife	naɪf
fire	faɪə	there's a	ðez ə
fruit	fruːt	are in **front** of	ər ɪn frʌnt əv
fly	flaɪ		

Unit 9   v (van)

Sound production

First practise f. Then use your voice to make v.

Student difficulties

This sound is difficult for speakers of Arabic, Japanese, Spanish, Chinese, Lao and Khmer. Some Dutch, Vietnamese, German, and Turkish speakers may also have some difficulty. The most common English sound with which v is replaced is f, particularly at the end of words. Japanese and Spanish speakers may replace it with b, Chinese with w. Contrast of the sound in isolation with f is helpful, especially with a physical demonstration of the lip position and a large blackboard sketch. Show use of the voice in v but not f. For students who replace v with w, contrast of these two sounds is also important.

Linking up with course work

EXERCISE I

They've got a television. Have they got a television? Yes, they have. / No, they haven't.

   Link with teaching on the verb 'to have'. Particularly if students have not already practised this with 'got' in their general course, use classroom realia

or selected flashcards from Unit 1 Exercise 1 and 3 (singular) as prompts to practise requests. For example:
Student A: Have you got a book?
Student B: Yes, I have. Here you are. / Sorry. No, I haven't.
   Note weak form of 'have' in the question: həv.

Suggested procedures

Minimal pair practice as relevant to students (see above):
f/v   fan/van; fine/vine; leaf/leave
b/v   berry/very; B/V; best/vest
w/v   Unit 10, Exercise 1, practising Sound 2 first.

EXERCISE 1

Note: In spoken English it is more usual to say, for example, 'I've got a pen' than 'I have a pen.'
   Weak form of *have* in questions: həv. Strong form of *have* in short answers: hæv, hævnt.
   Weak forms of: *are* ə; *a* ə; *of* əv; *some* səm.
   Linking of v and f sounds in: *have Victor*; *of fruit*; *of flowers*; *five fish*; *twelve forks*.

Steps
1 Students listen and repeat: *Victor, Vera, visitor, visiting, they're*, then repeat or read sentences below picture.
2 Students practise the following words from the blackboard: *have, five, of, twelve, eleven, very, vase*; then listen and repeat the two substitution lists at the end of this unit paying attention to the weak forms and linking sounds listed above.
3 Students practise short answers to the question, for example:
   Teacher: Have they got five fish?
   Student(s): No, they haven't.
4 Students practise the question, making substitutions, then begin pair practice as in the Example.

Further practice

1 Use pictures in Unit 7 Exercise 2 to practise, for example: It's a **ve**ry **he**avy **ba**by.
2 Link with teaching of the verb 'to give', for example, with flashcards: 'Give me a fork/flower/some wine/water.'

Spelling

The sound v is usually written with the letter 'v'.
Examples: (**B** = Beginner; **E** = Elementary) **B** television, very, visit,
visitor, heavy, seven, eleven, seventeen, seventy **E** never, over, river

Other spellings:
ve **B** give, have, five, twelve. **E** leave, live, love, move, evening, every
f of

Pronunciation of some words in this unit

a **bowl** of **fruit**   ə bəʊl əf fruːt
They've **got** some **flow**ers   ðeɪv gɒt səm flaʊəz
Have they **got** a te**le**vision?   həv ðeɪ gɒt ə telɪvɪʒn
Yes, they **have**.   jes ðeɪ hæv
No, they **haven't**.   nəʊ ðeɪ hævnt

Victor   vɪktə
Vera   vɪərə
visitors   vɪzɪtəz
vase   vɑːz
very   verɪ

Unit 10   w (window)

Sound production

This is close to the English sound u. Make your lips round and hard for w.
w is a short sound.

Student difficulties

Speakers of Dutch, German, Turkish, Farsi, Scandinavian languages,
Japanese, Hebrew, Spanish and Greek have difficulty with this sound.
German, Italian, Scandinavian and Turkish speakers replace w with v.
Dutch, Lao and Farsi speakers also confuse w and v or make an intermediate
sound for both. Spanish and Greek speakers may replace this sound with gw
or a similar sound. Hebrew speakers may confuse this sound with r. Japanese
sometimes replace w with a sound close to f. Speakers of Spanish, Japanese
and some other Asian languages have particular difficulty in pronouncing
this sound when it is followed by ʊ or uː. Seeing the correct lip position for
w through both physical demonstration and diagram is helpful for all
students. It may also help to practise saying uː before vowels and practise
saying this smoothly (e.g. you – uː – all – wall; you – uː – ill – will).

Linking up with course work

EXERCISES 2 AND 3

What's the weather like? It's wet.
What's the watch like? It's square.
   Link with physical descriptions, for example: 'What's your car/your house like?
   Also link with general teaching of 'wh' questions.

EXERCISE 3

Times: quarter/twenty past. Linking with telling the time: What's the time? quarter/twenty to.

Suggested procedures

EXERCISE 1

For suggested teaching procedures for minimal pairs, see page 104.
   Contrasts for further practice relevant to student difficulties:

v/w   V/we; vest/west; veal/wheel
f/w   fall/wall; fight/white; first/worst; full/wool
b/w   ball/wall; B/we; bell/well; bird/word

EXERCISE 2

Steps
1 Students listen and repeat the question and answers at the beginning of this exercise.
2 Students practise the answers in preparation for pair practice. With a mixed nationality class, ask the question about the students' country. With a single nationality class ask about different towns or regions known to the students.
3 Pair practice as in the Example.

EXERCISE 3

Steps
1 Students first practise words with consonant clusters, k + w, t + w: square, quiet, quarter, twenty, twelve.
2 Students listen and repeat the questions and answers at the beginning of this exercise.
3 Pair practice of telling the time, for example:
   Clock 1.
   Student A: What's the time?
   Student B: It's quarter past one.

Further practice

1 Repeat questions and answers in Unit 5 Exercise 2. Example: 'Which one is Sue's mother?' 'The one with the dog.'
2 Students choose the correct word to begin these questions about the picture in Unit 9.
   Which, what or where?
   1 ....woman has got a hat on? Fay.
   2 ....is under the table? A leaf.
   3 ....is the fruit? On the table.
   4 ....man has got a fork in his hand? Victor.
   5 ....is on Fred's head? A fly.

Spelling

The sound **w** is usually written with the letter 'w'.
Examples: ($\boxed{\text{B}}$ = Beginner; $\boxed{\text{E}}$ = Elementary)
$\boxed{\text{B}}$ twelve, twenty, warm, watch, we, weather, wet, wind, window, with, woman, word
$\boxed{\text{E}}$ between, sweet, swim, wait, walk, wall, want, way, water, wear, well, west, wide, wife, will, winter, wood, work, world, worse, worst

Other spellings:
wh $\boxed{\text{B}}$ what, when, where, which, white; $\boxed{\text{E}}$ why
qu   (pronounced kw) $\boxed{\text{B}}$ quarter, question, quiet, square; $\boxed{\text{E}}$ quick, queen
o   one, once

Pronunciation of some words in this unit

vine	vaɪn	warm	wɔːm
wine	waɪn	**w**indy	wɪndɪ
veil	veɪl	square	skweə
whale	weɪl	**qui**et	kwaɪət
weather	weðə	**quar**ter	kwɔːtə

Unit 11   ə (a camera)

Sound production and student difficulties

See notes on Unit 3.

Linking up with course work

This unit provides a review of three aspects of language introduced in Units 9 and 10:

EXERCISE I

Weak form of *of* in, for example: a vase of flowers. Link with teaching of short requests as given in a restaurant or shop, for example: a glass/bottle of milk/white wine, etc; a packet/tin/kilo of biscuits/tea etc.

EXERCISE 2

Weak form of *the* and *o* in *o'clock*. Link with telling the time, for example: Have you got a watch/the time? Yes, it's eleven o'clock.

EXERCISE 3

Weak form of *have* in questions. Link with structure teaching of this verb or with teaching of requests using this structure, for example: 'I want a pencil. Have you got one?' 'Yes, here you are.' Requests in a shop, for example: 'Have you got a tin of biscuits?' etc.

Suggested procedures

EXERCISE I

Steps
1 Students listen and repeat sentences for items 1, 3, 5, 7.
2 Students read the sentences and make sentences for items 2, 4, 6, 8.

EXERCISES 2 AND 3

Pair practice as in the Examples.

Further practice

Use of the verb 'have' in requests: Give the following items to students: a book, pen, pencil, ruler, piece of chalk, cigarette, match, coin, note.

Then ask, for example: Have you got a match, (please)? to elicit the response of giving the object to you. Then students practise the question and response with these objects. Note possible verbal responses: 'Here you are./ Sorry.'

Spelling

See Unit 3.

Unit 12 m (mouth)

Sound production

Close your lips. Use your voice. The sound m comes through your nose.

Student difficulties

Students generally do not have difficulty in pronouncing this sound, but Japanese, Spanish and Portuguese speakers confuse n with m at the end of words. Lao speakers may nasalise some vowels after m and n. This unit can be taught quickly in preparation for the next unit on n.

Linking up with course work

It is assumed here that students understand invitations using the verb 'to come'. If this has not yet been introduced in course work, students will probably have some understanding of this from invitations expressed in classroom instructions, for example: 'Come in'; 'Come here'; 'Come to the blackboard'.

Suggested procedures

Students listen and repeat words and sentences on the pictures, and then make sentences as in the Example. Note weak forms of: *to* tə, *the* ðə.

Further practice

Use the pictures in this unit to practise the longer, more polite form of invitation, for example: 'Would you like to come to the market?' Note rising intonation in this form.

Spelling

The sound m is written with the letter 'm'.
Examples: (B = Beginner; E = Elementary) B family, farm, me, man, meal, mother, room
E from, him, make, milk, small, stamp, swim

Other spellings:
me   B name, come, home, time E game, same
mn   autumn
mm   summer, swimming

Pronunciation of some words in this unit

market mɑːkɪt   home həʊm
swimming pool swɪmɪŋ puːl   come kʌm
farm fɑːm

Unit 13 n (nose)

Sound production

Touch the roof of your mouth with the tip of your tongue. Touch your side teeth with the sides of your tongue. Use your voice. n comes through your nose.

Student difficulties

At the end of words Spanish, Portuguese and Japanese speakers confuse n with m, while Chinese speakers may pronounce n close to ŋ. Greek students may omit this sound before 'd' or 't'. Some students may have difficulty with syllabic n in words like: seven sevn; lesson lesn; isn't ɪznt.

Linking up with course work

Link with a) teaching the time and times of day: in the morning/afternoon/ evening,
         b) practice of negative short answers containing words with syllabic n – *isn't, haven't, hasn't*. Students having difficulty with these will be likely to have the same problem later on with: *doesn't, didn't, couldn't, wouldn't, shouldn't*.

Suggested procedures

EXERCISE I

For suggested teaching procedures for minimal pairs, see page 104.
   Contrasts for further practice: some/sum; them/then; mine/nine; mummy/money; moon/noon.

EXERCISE 2

Note: Abbreviations a.m. (ante meridiem: before noon, i.e. times from midnight to midday); p.m. (post meridiem: afternoon, i.e. times from midday to midnight).
   The point of time when 'afternoon' changes to 'evening' is not clearly defined. Approximately 6.00 p.m. onwards is 'in the evening'.

Steps

1 Students listen and repeat numbers and times and answer the question 'What's the time?'
2 In the second section students are practising words with syllabic n. Note pronunciation: lesn/sevn/lɪsn/ɪlevn/sevnti:n/stju:dnts/sevntɪ/ɪznt. A simplified transcription of some words on the blackboard with stress shown should help students who find syllabic n difficult.

Example:

● •   ● •
lessn   **se**vn

● • •   ● •   ●● •
Lisn   to   **le**ssn   e**le**vn

EXERCISE 3

Steps

1 Students listen and repeat the words at the end of this exercise.
2 Students listen to the dialogue on tape or read by the teacher.
3 Students practise B's part in the dialogue. Show the contrast in intonation of these two questions with gestures and/or arrows on the blackboard. Teacher takes A's part, giving substitutions.
4 Students practise the dialogue in pairs after some examples have been done with the class listening.

Further practice

Syllabic n in short answers with *haven't, hasn't, isn't.*
Example: Short answers to questions about the picture in Unit 9:
1 Is Victor/Vera a visitor?
2 Has Vera got a hat/fly/flower on her head?
3 Has Fred got a fork/knife/piece of fruit/fly/bag/hat in his hand?
4 Have Victor and Vera got a television/a fan/a telephone/four visitors/five fish?

Spelling

The sound n is usually written with the letter 'n'.
Examples: (**B** = Beginner; **E** = Elementary) **B** name, number, policeman, moon, pen, cinema; **E** animal, many, minute, begin, run, thin

Other spellings:
kn   knife, know
nn   **B** funny, penny, Jenny, sunny, beginner; **E** beginning, running, thinner

ne   [B] one, nine, nineteen, ninety, aeroplane, telephone; [E] mine, none, sunshine

Syllabic n:

en   [B] listen, eleven, haven't, seven, seventeen, seventy, student; [E] garden, present, often

on   lesson, person

an   important

ion   television

Pronunciation of some words in this unit

mice	maɪs	lesson	lesn
nice	naɪs	seven	sevn
a.m.	eɪ em	eleven	ɪlevn
p.m.	pi: em	listen	lɪsn
morning	mɔːnɪŋ	students	stjuːdnts
afternoon	ɑːftənuːn	seventy	sevntɪ
evening	iːvnɪŋ	isn't	ɪznt

Unit 14   ŋ (ring)

Sound production

Touch the back of the roof of your mouth with the back of your tongue. Use your voice. ŋ comes through your nose.

Student difficulties

This sound occurs in few words in the beginners' vocabulary range. But once students learn the Present Continuous tense they will be using this sound very frequently, and although mistakes rarely cause confusion in meaning, they are very noticeable. Arabic, French, some German, Farsi, Hebrew, Italian, Spanish, Turkish and Slavic speakers have difficulty with this sound, pronouncing it ŋg, ŋk or n. For students who add g or k to this sound it sometimes helps to get them to sing the sound (for example: the word 'sing') and end it by gradually getting softer. It may also help to practise, for example, 'longer' or 'thinker' and gradually slow down the pronunciation and increase the gap between the first and second syllables.

Linking up with course work

Link with description of actions in the Present Continuous tense.

Suggested procedures

EXERCISE I

For suggested teaching procedures for minimal pairs, see page 104.
   Contrasts for further practice:
ŋk/ŋ bank/bang; wink/wing; rink/ring
n/ŋ   thin/thing; Ron/wrong; look in/looking; come in/coming, etc.

EXERCISE 2

Note: The purpose of this exercise is to practise word stress in verbs ending in
'ing'. As students will be concentrating on the sound ŋ in this unit, they may
tend to over-stress the last syllable of these words.

Steps
Students listen and repeat the words and phrases, reading the columns
vertically. Tap with a ruler to show stress patterns.

EXERCISE 3

Note: Joining of z and s sounds in: Mr Long is sleeping.

Steps
For students who have had little or no practice in the Present Continuous
tense:

First lesson

1 Students look at the picture and listen to sentences on tape or read by the
teacher: Ben is reading. Anne is washing her hair. Mr Long is sleeping.
Grandmother is drinking tea. Grandfather is watching television. Ron and
Dan are playing table tennis.
2 Students listen and repeat these sentences and/or finish sentences started by
the teacher.
3 Students make sentences as in *Example 1*.
4 Other sentences for further practice: Ben is eating an apple. The cat is
sleeping. Anne is listening to the radio and singing. Grandfather is
smoking a pipe. The telephone is ringing.

Second lesson

1 Students practise the 'wh' question, for example:
Teacher: Anne
Student(s): What's Anne doing?
Check falling intonation in these questions.
2 Students practise in pairs as in *Example 2*.
3 This can be extended to plural questions: 'What are Ron and Dan/
Grandmother and Grandfather/Mr Long and the cat doing?'

EXERCISE 4

Steps

1 Students listen to the dialogue on tape or read by the teacher. After practising Exercise 3 students should have no difficulty in understanding if they have already practised, 'Good morning. How are you?' and the reply.
2 Students read or repeat all or part of the dialogue.
3 Role playing using initially only the first four lines of the dialogue. Example: conversations between Mrs Young and Ron, Mrs Young and Grandmother, etc.

Further practice

The visual in Exercise 3 can be used to link up with other work on the Present Continuous tense for practice in negative sentences and other question forms.
Examples:
Mrs Long isn't watching television.
Mrs Long is cooking, isn't she? Yes, she is.
Mrs Long isn't sleeping, is she? No, she isn't.
Is Mrs Long cooking? Yes, she is.
Who's sleeping? Mr Long is.

Spelling

The sound ŋ is usually written with the letters 'ng'.
Examples: ($\boxed{B}$ = Beginner; $\boxed{E}$ = Elementary) $\boxed{B}$ evening, morning, ring, long, young, reading, singing; $\boxed{E}$ bring, ceiling, nothing, spring, strong, thing, wrong

Other spellings:
n   drink, ink, pink, think, sink
     angry, hungry, finger, England, English, stronger

Pronunciation of some words in this unit

sink	sɪŋk	her **hair**	hɜː heə
sing	sɪŋ	**lis**tening to the **ra**dio	lɪsnɪŋ tə ðə reɪdɪəʊ
sinking	sɪŋkɪŋ	Mr **Long**	mɪstə lɒŋ
singing	sɪŋɪŋ	Mrs **Young**	mɪsɪz jʌŋ
pipe	paɪp		

Unit 15 e (pen)

Sound production

First practise the sound ɪ. Then open your mouth a *little* more. e is a short sound.

Student difficulties

Most students do not have difficulty with this sound. However, speakers of Dutch, Farsi and Arabic may confuse it with ɪ, and Chinese speakers may confuse it with ə or ʌ.

Linking up with course work

Link with teaching of comparisons using the words *better/best*.

Suggested procedures

EXERCISE I

For suggested teaching procedures for minimal pairs, see page 104.

EXERCISE 2

Note: weak forms: *a* ə; *the* ðə; *than* ðən.

Steps
1 Students listen and repeat words and sentences at the beginning of this exercise.
2 Practise the questions and answers as in the two *Examples*. Note rising intonation in the question. Show stress pattern on the blackboard with weak stresses marked if students have difficulty with the weak form of *than*. Example:

•　●　●・　・　●
Is **Fred be**tter than **Ben**?

3 Pair practice of question and answers using the cues given in items 1–9.

EXERCISE 3

Note: Beginners may mispronounce letters of the alphabet because of confusion with their pronunciation in their own language. See suggestion under the heading *Extension* in Unit 6 Exercise 2.
  Pronunciation of letter z **zed**; American pronunciation zi:.

Further practice

Question and answer drill using the pictures in Unit 7 Exercise 2. *Example*:
picture 3:
Teacher: Is he heavy?
Student: Yes. He's very heavy.

Spelling

The sound e is usually written with the letter 'e'.
Examples: ($\boxed{\text{B}}$ = Beginner; $\boxed{\text{E}}$ = Elementary) $\boxed{\text{B}}$ pen, pencil, desk, lesson, twelve, twenty; $\boxed{\text{E}}$ dress, question, forget, remember, hotel, yesterday

Other spellings:
ea $\boxed{\text{B}}$ heavy, bread, weather; $\boxed{\text{E}}$ head, breakfast, already
a   any, many
ie   friend
ai   again

Pronunciation of some words in this unit

Betty	betɪ	**cle**ver	klevə
Jenny	dʒenɪ	thief	θiːf
better than	betə ðən		

Unit 16   æ (man)

Sound production

First practise the sound e. Then open your mouth a *little* more.

Student difficulties

Most students have difficulty with this sound. Dutch, German, Portuguese and Turkish speakers usually confuse it with e; French, Italian, Greek, Japanese and Spanish speakers and others may confuse it with ʌ. Chinese speakers confuse it with e and ʌ. Speakers of Slavic languages also have difficulty with this sound.

Linking up with course work

Use this unit to introduce or reinforce the structures 'They are all . . .' and 'except for . . .'
    If using the suggestions for further practice, link with practice of short answers using the words: *am, can, have, haven't, has, hasn't.*

Suggested procedures

EXERCISE 1

For suggested teaching procedures for minimal pairs see page 104.

Further practice of contrasts relevant to language groups above:

e/æ   M/am; men/man; bed/bad; end/ánd; head/had; send/sand

ʌ/æ   Unit 17 Exercise 1 (practising sound 2 first). Also: bud/bad; bug/bag; much/match

ɑː/æ First part of Unit 18 Exercise 1 (practising sound 2 first). Also: arm/am; bark/back; aunt/ant; aren't/ant; hard/had

EXERCISE 2

Steps

1 Students listen and repeat names and sentences in both parts of this exercise. Tap with a ruler to show stress patterns. Note that in section 1 students should take the same length of time to say names in the third column as in the first column. Similarly in section 2, although the sentences increase in length, all have four strong stresses and the last sentences should therefore be said in about the same length of time as the first.

2 Pair practice as in the *Example* using sentences from section 2. For beginners or weak students B's response can be limited to, for example: 'They are all very fat.'

3 Students may be able to make other sentences about the picture following this pattern: 'They are all standing/wearing black shoes/smiling except for Jack.'

Further practice

Several short answers which the students will have already practised have the sound æ.

1 Practise from the blackboard:

Short answers:

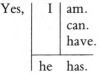

Yes, I am.
          can.
          have.
      he has.

No, I haven't.
      he hasn't.

2 Students give short answers to rapid oral questions. Choose questions at random from the three examples below or make questions relevant to the particular students:

a) Are you | studying English | ?
  | listening |
  | (student's name) |
  | (student's nationality) |
  | sitting next to Mr X |

b) Can you | understand | (student's language)?
  | speak |
  | read |
  | write |

c) Have you | got | a★ book |
   Has Mr X | | a pen | ?
  | | a pencil |

★Substitute words from the following list: a seat/a notebook/a ruler/a car/a bicycle/a watch/a cat/a television/a telephone/a farm/a swimming pool/an axe/an aeroplane

Spelling

The sound æ is always written with the letter 'a'.
Examples: ($\boxed{B}$ = Beginner; $\boxed{E}$ = Elementary) $\boxed{B}$ bag, family, fat, happy, hat, man; $\boxed{E}$ angry, bad, carry, match, stamp, taxi

Pronunciation of some words in this unit

N	en		**Pat**rick	pætrɪk
Anne	æn		**J**anet	dʒænət
X	eks		ex**cept** for	ɪksept fə
axe	æks		are **all**	ər ɔːl

Unit 17 ʌ (cup)

Sound production

First practise the sound æ. Then put your tongue back a little. ʌ is a very short sound.

Student difficulties

Many students have difficulty with this sound. Japanese, Turkish and German speakers may confuse it with æ. Dutch and French speakers usually

confuse it with ɜ:. Greek, Chinese and Lao speakers may confuse it with ɑ:.
Other students who can pronounce the sound ʌ are confused by the spelling
with the letter 'o' of so many words with this sound and say, for example,
lɒv instead of lʌv for the word 'love'.

Confusion is also caused because the sound is close to one which is spelt 'a'
in many European languages. Hence *cup* may be pronounced kæp and
spelling errors may also occur.

Linking up with course work

Link with teaching of family relationships: mother, brother, husband, etc.
Words not included in this unit: father, daughter, wife, sister, aunt,
grandfather, grand-daughter.

Students should be familiar with the possessive ' 's', for example: *Dan's book*.

Suggested procedures

EXERCISE 1

For suggested teaching procedures for minimal pairs, see page 104.
Further practice of contrasts relevant to language groups above:

æ/ʌ   bat/but; fan/fun; match/much; ran/run; track/truck
ɜ:/ʌ   Bert/but; shirt/shut; hurt/hut; bird/bud; girl/gull

EXERCISE 2

Note: Students find some words for family relationships difficult if these are
classified differently in their own language. Likely difficulties: in English an
uncle is your mother or father's brother OR the husband of your mother or
father's sister. A cousin is your aunt or uncle's child (same word for a boy or
a girl).

Students may also have difficulty if their naming system is different from
the English one of first name/surname (father's family name).

Weak forms: and ənd; are ə; has həz.

Steps
1 Practise pronunciation of names at the beginning of this exercise and
   check understanding by asking, for example: 'What's your first name/
   surname?' 'Is Andrew a boy's name or a girl's name?' etc.
2 If you expect students will have difficulty in understanding the family
   tree, begin by drawing the family tree on the blackboard while explaining
   and questioning. For example, Andrew Young is married to Anne Love.
   Anne is Andrew's wife. Andrew is Anne's husband. They have two
   children, Patrick and Patsy. Patrick is Andrew's son. Who is Patrick's
   mother? Who is Andrew's son? Who is Anne Love's husband? Who is
   Patsy Young's brother?

3 Students listen and repeat the words below the family tree. Check understanding of these words and if necessary explain with reference to the family tree.

4 Students complete the sentences at the end of this exercise. Note that all the sentences have five strong stresses and should therefore be read in the same length of time. The sentences can be used to practise this.

Example: Item 1.

Student A: Patsy Young is Dan Monday's mother.

Teacher: (Taps strong stresses with ruler to show length of time)

Students: (Repeat sentence while teacher taps again. Students say the sentence with this speed and rhythm).

Further practice

Make a blackboard list using students' suggestions from known vocabulary of words spelt with the letter 'o' but pronounced ʌ.

Words from this unit: love, young, London, Monday, mother, brother, son, money, another, one, doesn't, cousin, country

Other words at this level: nothing, honey, glove, colour, month, once, other, come, none, does

Spelling

The sound ʌ is usually written with the letter 'u'.

Examples: (B = Beginner; E = Elementary) B bus, cup, sun, up, under, husband; E funny, gun, jump, run, shut, understand

Other spellings:

o   (See words listed under *Further practice*)

ou   country, cousin, young

oe   does

Pronunciation of some words in this unit

Andrew ændru:	**hus**band hʌzbənd
Patsy pætsɪ	**un**cle ʌŋkl
Sally sælɪ	**cou**sin kʌzn
Love lʌv	a**no**ther ənʌðə
London lʌndən	**coun**try kʌntrɪ
Monday mʌndɪ	**te**legram telɪgræm
family fæm(ɪ)lɪ	

Unit 18 ɑː (heart)

Sound production

Put your tongue down and back. ɑː is a long sound.

Student difficulties

Many students have difficulty in making this long sound and substitute a shorter vowel.

Linking up with course work

Practice of short answers: Yes, I can./No, I can't; Yes, they are./No, they aren't.

Suggested procedures

EXERCISE I

For suggested teaching procedures for minimal pairs, see page 104.
    Further practice of contrasts relevant to language groups above:

æ/ɑ   am/arm; back/bark; ant/aunt; ant/aren't; had/hard
ʌ/ɑ   duck/dark; much/March; come/calm; putty/party
ɒ/ɑ   cot/cart; hot/heart; pot/part; box/barks; shop/sharp
ɜː/ɑ   firm/farm; stir/star; heard/hard; burn/barn

EXERCISE 2

Note: Pronunciation of *can*: in Yes/No questions, kæn or weak form kən; in the affirmative short answer, kæn. Pronunciation of *can't*: kɑːnt.
    Pronunciation of *are*: in Yes/No questions ɑː or weak form ə; in the affirmative short answer ɑː. Pronunciation of *aren't*: ɑːnt.

Steps
1 Students listen and repeat words and dialogue in the picture, then read the text below the picture. If students have difficulty in making the sound ɑː long enough, practise words from the blackboard with modified spelling: Grandfaaather, Chaaarles, Aaaunt, graaass, banaaanas, tomaaatoes, plaaants, glaaasses, caaan't.
2 Question and answer pair work using the words for substitution.

Extension: Students can learn to say 'Pardon?' as a request for repetition. Practise questions and answers, for example:
Student A: Are the glasses on the table?
Student B: Pardon?
Student A: Are the glasses on the table?
Student B: Yes, they are.

Further practice

Practice of short answers with *can/can't*. Students give answers to rapid oral questions:

Can	you	speak	(name languages	?
	Miss X	read	known/not known	
	Mr Z	write	by students)	
	people in (name country)	understand		
	any students in this class			

Spelling

The sound ɑː is usually written with the letter 'a'.
Examples: (**B** = Beginner; **E** = Elementary) **B** afternoon, answer, ask, can't, class, example, father, glass, grass, plant; **E** after, dance, last, nasty, fast

Other spellings:

ar   **B** are(n't), pardon, farm, garden, market, star; **E** dark, hard, large, party, March

au   aunt

ear   heart

al   half

Pronunciation of some words in this unit

cart	kɑːt	**as**king	ɑːskɪŋ
heart	hɑːt	**an**swering	ɑːnsərɪŋ
Uncle **Charles**	ʌŋkl tʃɑːlz	**aren't**	ɑːnt
Aunt Ann	ɑːnt æn	Can you	kən ju
Grandfather	grændfɑːðə	I **can**	aɪ kæn
ba**na**nas	bənɑːnəz	I **can't**	aɪ kɑːnt
to**ma**toes	təmɑːtəʊz		

Unit 19   h (hat)

Sound production

Push a lot of air out very quickly. Do *not* touch the roof of your mouth with your tongue.

Student difficulties

This sound occurs very frequently at beginner level in words like *he*, *his*, etc. and it is very difficult for some students.

Group 1

Hebrew, Italian, French and Portuguese speakers tend to omit this sound and/or put it in front of words beginning with a vowel. Putting h in the wrong place seems to increase as students get more worried about not being able to say this sound. If students are getting to this stage, it may help to remind them that some native English speakers never pronounce it!

Group 2

Greek, Slavic and Spanish speakers pronounce h like the sound x in *loch*. For these students:

a) Emphasize that the tongue is not used.

b) Show that it is like panting hard after running.

c) Show that a lot of air is needed to make this sound. Hold a strip of paper in front of your mouth, and make the sounds x and h to show the difference in effect.

Group 3

Japanese speakers confuse the sound h with f before most vowels but confuse it with ʃ before the sounds iː or ɪ. Chinese speakers also confuse the sounds s, ʃ and h initially before the sounds iː or ɪ. This difficulty will be particularly noticeable in distinguishing the words *he* and *she*. Students in Group 2 may also share this difficulty.

Linking up with course work

Link with a) practice of known question forms beginning with this sound: How much …? How many …? How often …? Who …? Whose …? Exercise 2 provides practice in questions beginning with *whose* and answers with possessive pronouns *his/hers*.

            b) practice of the greeting 'Hello. How are you?' and answers to this type of question: 'Fine/All right/Very well/OK.'

Suggested procedures

EXERCISE 1

For suggested teaching procedures for minimal pairs, see page 104.

     Note that this contrast is helpful for both groups of students who have difficulty with this sound. Further practice: at/hat; and/hand; air/hair; ear/here; old/hold; Ow!/how. Minimal pair sentences with this contrast are rare, and for this reason omission of the sound h seldom causes misunderstanding in meaning at sentence level.

EXERCISE 2

Steps
1 Students listen and repeat the words in the pictures.
2 Students practise the questions, for example:
    Teacher: handbag.
    Student: Whose handbag is this?
    Teacher: It's hers.
3 Pair practice as in the *Example*
4 The answer can be extended if students already know: Give it to him/her;
    Give him his horse/ Give her her elephant.

EXERCISE 3

Note: Stress and intonation change in the second 'How are you?' The weak
form of *are* ə is used here.
    Pronunciation of *your* jɔ:, *your uncle* jɔ:r ʌŋkl. In rapid speech this is often
shortened to: jə, jər.

Steps
1 Students listen to the dialogue on tape or read by the teacher.
2 Practise answers to the question 'How are you?'
3 Students read or repeat the dialogue, then practise in pairs.
4 Words for substitution can be extended to include: wife, husband,
    mother, son, etc. Check the distinction in pronunciation between he/she.

EXERCISE 4

Steps
1 If necessary introduce vocabulary items: old, unhappy, afraid, hospital,
    operation, hurt, a bath, a nurse.
2 Students listen to the joke on tape or read by the teacher, then practise
    reading it.

Further practice

Use the picture in Unit 14 Exercise 3 (Student's Book) to practise questions
with 'who'. *Example*: 'Who's watching television?'
    Link up with teaching of formal introductions using 'How do you do?'
(See Unit 40.)

Spelling

The sound h is written with the letter 'h'.
Examples: (B = Beginner; E = Elementary) B have, hello, happy,
home, house, horse; E behind, heavy, hold, help, hotel, how.

Other spellings:
wh who, whose

Pronunciation of some words in this unit

high	haɪ	operation	ɒpəreɪʃn
elephant	eləfnt	unhappy	ʌnhæpɪ
apple	æpl	afraid	əfreɪd
whose	huːz	nurse	nɜːs
hello	heləʊ	bath	bɑːθ
fine	faɪn	arrives	əraɪvz
all **right**	ɔːl raɪt	hurt	hɜːt
hospital	hɒspɪtl		

Unit 20 ɒ (clock)

Sound production

First practise the sound æ. Then put your tongue slightly back and bring your lips slightly forward. ɒ is a short sound.

Student difficulties

This sound is not a major problem, but most students will benefit from practising it in contrast with æ, ʌ and ɑː as the pronunciation of ɒ may be close to these.

Linking up with course work

Link up with a)   teaching of requests in a shop using 'Have you got ...?' and 'I want a ...'.
         b)   practice of 'a lot of'.

Suggested procedures

EXERCISE I

For suggested teaching procedures for minimal pairs, see page 104.
   Contrasts for further practice:
æ/ɒ   Anne/on; tap/top; backs/box; black/block; Larry/lorry
ʌ/ɒ   nut/not; bus/boss; gun/gone; shut/shot; run/Ron
ɑː/ɒ   sharp/shop; barks/box; part/pot; last/lost

EXERCISE 2

Students practise the question and answer about each of the shops.

EXERCISE 3

Students listen to the dialogue on tape or read by the teacher, then practise in pairs.

Note: Weak form of *have* həv and *of* əv in Exercises 2 and 3.

Further practice

Practice of requests (see *Further Practice* for Unit 11.) *Example*:
A: Have you got a pen?
B: Here you are./Sorry, I haven't got one.

Spelling

The sound ɒ is written with the letter 'o'.
Examples: ($\boxed{B}$ = Beginner; $\boxed{E}$ = Elementary) $\boxed{B}$ box, dog, got, shop, not, on; $\boxed{E}$ copy, doctor, drop, hot, long, stop.

Other spellings:
a: want, watch, wash, what
au: because, sausage

Pronunciation of some words in this unit

sack	sæk	**wa**tches	wɒtʃiz
sock	sɒk	**cu**stomer	kʌstəmə
what	wɒt	**shop** assistant	ʃɒp əsistənt
want	wɒnt	a **lot** of	ə lɒt əv

Unit 21 ɔː (ball)

Sound production

First practise the sound ɒ. Then put the back of your tongue up a *little*. ɔː is a long sound.

Student difficulties

Many students have difficulty with this sound, usually making it too short and confusing it with ɒ. Where the letter 'r' forms part of the spelling of this sound most students pronounce this when it should be silent. (See Unit 26: silent r.)

Linking up with course work

Link with practice in describing things and people using words: large/small; tall/short; long/short.

Suggested procedures

EXERCISE 1

For suggested teaching procedures for minimal pairs, see page 104.
   Further practice of this contrast: spot/sport; not/nought; shot/short.

EXERCISES 2 AND 3

Note: In normal sentence stress both adjective and noun are stressed with major stress on the noun, for example: It's a **large ball**. But when the adjectives are contrasted (as in Exercise 2) major stress is usually on the adjective, for example: It's a **large ball**./It's a **small ball**. In Exercise 3 the adjectives are not contrasted and major stress is on the noun, for example: a **small door**.

EXERCISE 2

Steps

1 Students practise sentences using the words *large/small* with normal sentence stress. Sketch the following on the blackboard to elicit sentences:

It's a **large cat**./small dog/large box/small clock/large sock/small pot/large fork/small fox. (If you can't draw and the sketches are very bad, students will feel more confident about drawing in Exercise 3!)
2 Students listen and repeat the pairs of sentences in the first half of this exercise. Stress: It's a **large ball**.
3 Students make sentences about the second set of pictures: He's a tall/short doctor. It's a small/large box. It's a long/short piece of chalk.

EXERCISE 3

Steps

1 Students read or repeat the first four descriptions corresponding to the pictures. Each item has four stressed syllables and all should therefore be

said in about the same length of time. Tap with a ruler to help students practise this.

2 Choose an item at random from the list of things to draw and sketch it rapidly on the blackboard. Students say what it is, for example: That's a tall glass with a little water in it.

3 Ask students to draw the other items. (Show each student which item to draw from the list as the other students should not know which one he is drawing.) Other students identify the drawing from the list.

Further practice

a) Link up with practice of the greeting: Good morning.

b) Telling the time: *quarter to*, *quarter past*. Repeat items 1–4 in Unit 10 Exercise 3 and give further examples.

Spelling

The sound ɔ: is written with many different spellings, usually containing the letter 'a' or 'o':
(**B** = Beginner; **E** = Elementary)

a	**B** all, ball, wall, water, small; **E** already, call
ar	warm, quarter
al	chalk, walk, talk
au	August, autumn
aw	draw, awful
o	story
or	**B** fork, forty, horse, morning, or, short; **E** corner, important, north
our	your, four, fourteen, pour
oor	door, floor
ore	more, before
ure	sure

Pronunciation of some words in this unit

Dawn	dɔːn	warm	wɔːm
port	pɔːt	**wa**ter	wɔːtə
fox	fɒks	bath	bɑːθ
forks	fɔːks	**foot**baller	fʊtbɔːlə
large	lɑːdʒ	chalk	tʃɔːk
small	smɔːl	a **lot** of	ə lɒt əv
short	ʃɔːt	a **piece** of	ə piːs əv
doctor	dɒktə		

Unit 22   ə (a camera)

Sound production and student difficulties

See notes on Unit 3.

    Words ending in the letters 'er' usually end with the sound ə. Many students have difficulty with this sound when the next word begins with a vowel and the letter 'r' is pronounced.

Linking up with course work

Link with a)   practice of weak forms of *and* and *but*,
          b)   practice of requests using the weak form of *can*. (See examples under *Further practice*.)

Suggested procedures

EXERCISE 1

Note: This exercise gives practice in making the sound ə with the letter 'r' pronounced before a vowel. This introduces the problem of pronounced and silent 'r' which will be met in Unit 27.

    Pronunciation of *your*: jɔ:. Can be shortened to jə in rapid speech.

Steps

1 Students practise the words at the beginning of this exercise.
2 Practise these words using the pictures numbered 1–10. *Example*: 1 brʌðə
   2 brʌðər ənd sistə/sistər ənd brʌðə.
3 Students make questions for items 1–10 as in the Examples.

EXERCISE 2

Note: In Unit 18 students practised short answers using *can/can't*. Here the same situation is used to practise questions with the weak form of *can*: kən.
    Weak form of *but* bət in the riddles. Weak form of *of* əv in the answers.

Steps

1 Students first look at the picture in Unit 18 Exercise 2, and give short answers to questions asked by the teacher, for example: 'Can he/grandfather see, walk, run?' etc.
2 Students look at the pictures in Unit 22 Exercise 2 and practise the questions.
3 Students practise in pairs, role playing: Aunt Ann, Grandfather.

Further practice

Practice of requests for food. *Examples*:
a) Can I have some *water/butter/pepper, please?
    ★ *Substitute*: water and ice; butter and jam; pepper and salt.
b) *A*: Can I have *an apple, please?
    B: Yes, of course.
    A: Can I have another apple, please?
    B: Sorry. There aren't any more apples.
    ★ *Substitute*: an orange, a biscuit, an egg, a cake, an onion, an icecream, a banana.
Note: Weak forms: *can* kən; *have* həv; *some* səm; *a* ə; *an* ən; *of* əv; *there* ðər.
    Pronunciation of 'r' before vowels in *another*, *more*, *there*.

Spelling

(See Unit 3.)

Pronunciation of some words in this unit

television	telɪˈvɪʒn	**ri**ddle	rɪdl
listen	lɪsn	a**no**ther	ənʌðə(r)
radio	reɪdjəʊ		

Unit 23 ɜ: (girl)

Sound production

First practise the sound ɔ:. Then put your tongue forward and up a little. ɜ: is a long sound.

Student difficulties

Many students have difficulty with this sound, confusing it with ɔ:, e, ʌ or ɑ:. When the sound is written *ir*, *er* or *ur*, students tend to try to pronounce the vowel and the 'r'. It is often helpful to emphasise that the lips should be spread by asking students to begin by making a sad face with the lips turned down at the corners to make this sound.

Linking up with course work

Link up with practice of the Simple Present tense in talking about daily work routine (see *Further practice*).

Suggested procedures

EXERCISE I

For suggested teaching procedures for minimal pairs, see page 104.

Further practice of contrasts relevant to students' difficulties mentioned above:

ɔ:/ɜ: warm/worm; blackboard/blackbird; four/fur; call/curl

e/ɜ: bed/bird; west/worst; ten/turn; Ben/burn

ʌ/ɜ: shut/shirt; but/Bert; bud/bird; bun/burn

ɑ:/ɜ: barn/burn; far/fur; Carl/curl; Pa/purr

EXERCISE 2

Note: Change in pronunciation of *the* before a vowel in the proverb: ði: ɜ:li bɜ:d; ðə wɜ:m.

Weak form: *that* ðət.

Steps

1 Students repeat words and sentences in the picture.
2 Discussion of the meaning of the proverb appropriate to students' level, for example: People who get up early in the morning are more successful or make more money.
3 Students learn and practise saying the proverb.

EXERCISE 3

Note: If students have not yet learnt the Simple Present tense, check their understanding of meaning here, for example: Picture 1: It's (say present time) o'clock now. Pearl isn't getting up now. But she gets up at 6.30 every morning (blackboard: Monday √ Tuesday √ Wednesday √ etc.)

Weak forms: *at* ət; *a* ə; *and* ənd; *to* tə; *the* ðə.

A working girl (main stress on *working*): a young woman who goes to work.

Steps. Students:

1 listen to the narrative on tape or read by the teacher, first with books closed then repeat with books open,
2 read aloud or repeat the narrative,
3 answer questions with short answers.

Examples:

Is Pearl a student or a working girl? (a working girl)

Does Pearl get up late or early? (early)

Does she get up at 6.30 or 7.30? (6.30)

Is she hungry or thirsty in the morning? (thirsty)

Does she put on a long shirt or a short shirt? (a short shirt)

Does she put on a long skirt or a short skirt? (a long skirt)
What time does she walk to work? (7.30)
What time does she arrive at work? (8.30)
Is Pearl the third person or the first person at work? (the first person)

Further practice

Students talk about daily work routine. *Example*:
My father works in a ....
He starts work at .... in the morning.
He walks/doesn't walk to work.
Make these sentences appropriate to the student's age and circumstances, for example, working adults talk about their own routine, housewives about their husband's routine, etc.

Spelling

The sound ɜ: is usually written with the letters 'ir'.
Examples: bird, first, girl, shirt, skirt, thirsty, thirty, thirteen, dirty

Other spellings:
or   work, worm, world, worse, worst
er   her, person, weren't
ear early, learn, year
ur   Thursday, nurse, church

Pronunciation of some words in this unit

Paul	pɔːl	worm	wɜːm
Pearl	pɜːl	**ear**ly	ɜːlɪ
shorts	ʃɔːts	**cat**ches	kætʃɪz
shirts	ʃɜːts	ar**riv**es	əraɪvz
walks	wɔːks	**per**son	pɜːsn
works	wɜːks	**pro**verb	prɒvɜːb
warm	wɔːm		

Unit 24   l (letter, ball)

Sound production

Clear l (letter): First practise n. To make l the air goes over the sides of your tongue and out of your mouth.

Dark l (ball): the middle of your tongue is slightly lowered to make this sound.

Student difficulties

Speakers of Lao and Vietnamese have great difficulty in distinguishing n and l at the end of words.

Some students find syllabic l difficult (words like *apple* æpl; *bottle* bɒtl).

Some students make no distinction between the two different l sounds in English:

clear l (followed by a vowel, for example: *letter, lovely*)

dark l (final sound or followed by a consonant, for example: *ball, old*).

Use of only one of these sounds causes no confusion in meaning, but contributes to an accent different from that of a native English speaker. Teachers therefore may or may not expect students to make the distinction between these two sounds, depending on whether the student's aim is to speak like a native English speaker or to be understood.

Linking up with course work

Link up with use of adjectives in descriptions. Adjectives used in this unit: yellow, black, blue, lovely, clean, clever, slow, small, full, old, cold, little, difficult.

Suggested procedures

Note: Exercises for Sound A provide practice in clear l, those for Sound B dark l. Exercise 3 provides practice in both.

Sound A EXERCISE 1

For suggested teaching procedures for minimal pairs, see page 104.

Contrasts for further practice: not/lot; no/low; snow/slow.

EXERCISE 2

Students listen and repeat each item.

Note: Students may find part (ii) of this exercise more difficult as this contains examples of l in consonant clusters. If necessary practise from the blackboard, for example:

llllower fllllower flower: llllack, bllllack, black.

Main stress on the final word in each item, for example: a **le**mon **je**lly:

a **ye**llow **te**lephone as in normal sentence stress for adjective + noun (see notes on Unit 21 Exercises 2–3).

Note that two nouns are used as adjectives here: *lemon, colour*.

Sound B EXERCISE 1

Contrasts for further practice: ten/tell; win/will; mine/mile; rain/rail.

EXERCISE 2

Students listen and repeat each item.
Note: Section (i) – dark I in final position. Section (ii) – dark I in consonant clusters. (Here ignore any mispronunciation of the sound əʊ in the words *old*, *cold* as this sound with dark I seems a particularly difficult combination.) Section (iii) – syllabic I. Writing these words in modified phonetic script on the blackboard may help, for example: **appl͵ peo**pl, **bi**cycl, etc. However, if students tend to pronounce this as clear I and do not make a syllable of the sound, write: **appəl, peo**pəl, **bi**cycəl, etc. Show word stress on the blackboard and check that students do not stress the final syllable in these words. Tapping word stress with a ruler may help here.

EXERCISE 3

Note: In the second sentence of each pair of practice items students are practising the final consonant cluster ɪz. Examples in the second column are more difficult as these are final clusters with three or more consonants: baɪsɪklz, ænɪmlz, teɪblz, pju:plz, ɪgzɑ:mplz, penslz. If necessary practise these from the blackboard first in modified phonetic script, for example: bicycls, animls, tabls etc. *or* bicycəls, animəls, tabəls etc.
   Pronunciation of *are all* ər ɔ:l.

Steps. Students:
1 read the sentences in items 1–12,
2 practise plurals: meals, balls, girls, etc.,
3 practise B's sentence in the Example,
4 make B's sentence for each item,
5 practise in pairs as in the Example.

Further practice

Students practise saying what they like/don't like, making sentences beginning: I don't like/don't mind/like/love ....

large	aeroplanes/televisions/pencils/pills/hotels/flowers
black	walls/telephones/glasses/plates/tables/bicycles
cold	meals/schools/apples/milk/hotels/people
clever	people/pupils/animals/children/girls.

Example:
Blackboard cue: large
Teacher: hotels
Student: I don't like large hotels.

Spelling

The sound I is written with the letter 'l'.
Examples: like, love, clever, cold, girl, twelve.

Other spellings: (B = Beginner; E = Elementary)
le   apple, example, little, people, bicycle, middle, smile, hole
ll   B all, ball, full, hello, hill, ill, wall, well, yellow, spell; E call, follow,
     pull, really, shall, shell, tell, will
doubling l   careful – carefully.

Pronunciation of some words in this unit

light	laɪt	apple	æpl
line	laɪn	pupil	pju:pl
Jenny	dʒenɪ	people	pi:pl
jelly	dʒelɪ	example	ɪgzɑ:mpl
lemon	lemən	bottle	bɒtl
colour	kʌlə	table	teɪbl
lovely	lʌvlɪ	pencil	pensl
clever	klevə	bicycle	baɪsɪkl
Bill	bɪl	little	lɪtl
hotel	həʊtel	animal	ænɪml

Unit 25   r (rain)

Sound production

Turn the tip of your tongue up and slightly back. Do not touch the roof of
your mouth. The sides of your tongue should touch your back teeth.

Student difficulties

Most students have some difficulty with the sound r.

Speakers of many Asian languages confuse l and r, particularly Japanese,
Lao and Chinese speakers.

French, German, Hebrew and Portuguese speakers often make a sound
which is too far back (uvular r).

Many students trill r, for example: speakers of Arabic, Italian, Greek,
Spanish, Turkish and Slavic languages.

Nearly all students pronounce r where it should be silent. This is a reading
difficulty rather than a pronunciation one, and is dealt with in the next two
units.

A trilled r does not cause any difficulties in understanding, and English
speakers are used to this in, for example, a Scottish accent. But repeated
blackboard work will help to draw students' attention to this problem, for
example: Not RRRRoad but road (with the letter 'r' of the second *road*
drawn very lightly). Point out that the English r is a very quiet sound.

Uvular r also causes no misunderstanding in meaning. But the sound r occurs so frequently that it is very difficult to listen to English pronounced in this way. Demonstration of the correct tongue position and practice of the l/r minimal pairs should help students to use the front of the tongue rather than the back.

Confusion of l *and* r causes very many misunderstandings in meaning. In demonstrating the tongue position emphasize that the tongue must not touch the roof of the mouth for r. This seems to be more difficult when r is in consonant clusters.

Linking up with course work

Link with descriptions of actions using the Present Continuous tense.

Suggested procedures

Note: The letter 'r' is always pronounced in all the words used in this unit. Check students' understanding of the rule at the beginning of the unit. Some students like to learn with a rule, but others learn only through practice.

EXERCISE 1

For suggested teaching procedures for minimal pairs, see page 104.
Contrasts for further practice: led/red; light/right; lane/rain; collect/correct;
flute/fruit; flame/frame; fly/fry; play/pray; cloud/crowd.

EXERCISE 2

Note: Possible difference in meaning between 'road' and 'street': a road usually goes between towns; a street is in a town.
Abbreviations for road (Rd.) and street (St.) are used only in the names.
The words 'truck' and 'lorry' have the same meaning in British English. In American English only truck is used.
Section B practises r in consonant clusters.

Steps: Question and answer pair work.
Examples:
1 Questions as in Student's Book and short answers.
2 Q: What's Ron doing?
   A: He's running along the street.
3 Q: Is Jenny throwing a ball along the street?
   A: No, she isn't. She's dropping fruit.
4 Q: Ross isn't driving a lorry along the street, is he?
   A: No, he isn't. He's practising football.
5 (omit Ron) Q: What's Jenny carrying?
   A: A television.

Further practice

Using students' suggestions, make a blackboard list from known vocabulary of words with 'r' which is always pronounced. Words at this level not included in this lesson: red, rich, right, round, repeat, rest, ring, aeroplane, story, tomorrow, orange, very.

Words in consonant clusters: train, address, dress, present, bread, crowd, April, February, Friday, Brazil, Africa, Britain, try, drink, break, cry, strong, dry, grey, green, across, three, through, from, front, every

Spelling

The sound r is written with the letter 'r'.
Examples: See list of words in *Further practice* (above).

Other spellings:
rr   tomorrow, carry, lorry, narrow
wr   write, wrong

Pronunciation of some words in this unit

wrong	rɒŋ	**An**drew	ændru:
jelly	dʒelɪ	**throw**ing	θrəʊɪŋ
Jenny	dʒenɪ	**lorry**	lɒrɪ
Mary	meərɪ	**prac**tising	præktɪsɪŋ
Riverall	rɪverɔ:l	**watering**	wɔ:tərɪŋ

Unit 26   silent r (girl)

Note: This unit provides practice of words in which 'r' is always silent. It also reviews the vowel sounds: ɔ:, ɑ:, ɜ:, ə.

Student difficulties

In some varieties of English (for example, American, Scottish) the letter 'r' is always pronounced, but students learning Received Pronunciation English find it difficult to know when not to pronounce 'r'.

Linking up with course work

EXERCISE 1

Link up with teaching of adjectives and practice of expressing surprise in exclamations, for example: Look at that/Just look at that/What a/Isn't that a dirty garden!

EXERCISE 2

Link up with students' requests in class for explanation of word meaning, for example: I don't understand/Could you please explain/Would you please explain/What's the meaning of the word 'north'?

Suggested procedures

Check students' understanding of the rule at the beginning of this unit in the Students' Book, for example: silent (not pronounced, has no sound), before consonants (p, b, l, m, n, etc.). As mentioned in Unit 25, some students prefer to learn with a rule, but others do not.

EXERCISE 1

Note: In these sentences students are practising the normal [adjective + noun] stress and intonation pattern where main stress is on the noun.

Steps: In each section students first repeat the words on the pictures, then choose the correct word to make sentences as in the Examples.

EXERCISE 2

Note: The list of words in this exercise provides the opportunity for review of word stress patterns.

Steps
1 Students read the text and then practise the sentence, 'I don't understand the word ....'.
   Explain any words students use to make this more meaningful.
2 Review of vowels ɔ:, ɑ:, ɜ:, ə. Write the thirteen words on the blackboard thus:

fourteen	arm	thirty	yesterday
forty	dark	worse	exercise
north	party	hers	forget
important			

Ask students which sound is repeated in each word, for example, in *Column 1*: ɔ:. After practising these words, students find other words in this unit with the same sound, and add these to the list for practice (morning, horse, warm, short, fork).
Column 2: ɑ: (afternoon, hard, large, garden, card, farm, carpet, market)
Column 3: ɜ: (worst, Thursday, Irma, learning, working, thirteen, words, first, world, bird, girl, church, thirsty, dirty, birthday)
Column 4: ə (Saturday, afternoon, understand, Irma, afternoon)

Further practice

Other words at this level in which the letter 'r' is always silent: dark, exercise, hers, person, quarter (the first 'r' is always silent), stairs, tired, careful.

Encourage students to mark any new words like this in their vocabulary lists, for example, with the symbol S.

Spelling

See notes on spelling of the sounds ɔ: (Unit 21), ɑ: (Unit 18), 3: (Unit 23), ə (Unit 3).

Pronunciation of some words in this unit

silent	saɪlənt	**Thurs**day	θ3:zdɪ
vowel	vaʊl	under**stand**	ʌndəstænd
church	tʃ3:tʃ	world	w3:ld
thirsty	θ3:stɪ	worse	w3:s
carpet	kɑ:pɪt	**yes**terday	jestədɪ
fork	fɔ:k	for**get**	fəget
Irma	3:mə	im**por**tant	ɪmpɔ:tnt
worst	w3:st	north	nɔ:θ
Saturday	sætədɪ		

Unit 27   r/silent r (her apples/her books)

Student difficulties

Students have a lot of difficulty with words ending in 'r' or 're' as the pronunciation changes if the next word begins with a vowel. This has already been practised in Unit 22 Exercise 1: 'That's my mother (mʌðə).' but 'That's my mother (mʌðər) and father.' Students need a lot of this kind of practice before correct pronunciation becomes automatic.

Linking up with course work

Link up with teaching and practice of:
- possessive pronouns: her, your, our, their;
- descriptions of location using: over there, near, in, at, under, next to, behind, in front of.

Suggested procedures

EXERCISE I

Steps: Students read or repeat the words on the pictures, then practise the three sentence patterns with the pictures. If students have a lot of difficulty, group the words on the blackboard and practise from this first:

A	B
pencils	apples
books	eggs
flowers	icecreams
	oranges
	umbrellas

EXERCISE 2

Note: The final 'r' in words in columns 2 and 4 is pronounced when the next word begins with a vowel.

Steps

1 Ask students to cover column 5 with a book, and column 3 with a pen or strip of paper. Practise sentences using words from columns 1, 2 and 4 only, for example: That's our teacher.
2 Students uncover column 3. Check understanding of vocabulary. Practise sentences using columns 1, 2, 3 and 4, for example: That's their English teacher.
3 Students uncover column 5. Check understanding. Practise sentences using words from all columns as in the Example. Note that all sentences have five main stresses; although the sentences vary in length they should be said in about the same length of time. Tap with a ruler to show main stresses.
4 After practice in reading these sentences, students can be asked to make sentences from cue words in column 3 and demonstration from column 5.
   Example:
   Teacher: (stands under the light) funny
   Student(s): That's our funny teacher under the light!

Further practice

Students practise sentences from:

	mother	understands this
	father	is very angry
My	sister	sings well
	brother	eats a lot
	doctor	likes music
	teacher	asks too many questions

Spelling

Students often have difficulty in spelling words ending in 'r' or 're' as there is no sound r at the end to help them when the word is practised in isolation or before a consonant. Students should hear these words both in isolation and in a sentence where the next word begins with a vowel. If possible construct sentences for the students using the words in brackets:

'er' words
another (apple); better (eggs); letter (A); number (8); quarter (of an hour); remember (it); summer (and winter); under (a tree); water (in a cup); weather (is fine); paper (and pencils)

're' words
where (is the); here (it is); there (are some); picture (of a)

other words
star (in the sky); for (everybody); door (is open); floor (is dirty); dear (old lady); near (a town); hear (it); chair (over there); wear (a hat)

Pronunciation of some words in this unit

silent	saɪlənt	umbrellas	ʌmbreləz
her	hɜ:	your	jɔ:
pronounced	prənaʊnst	our	ɑ:
vowel	vaʊl	their	ðeə
Mary	meərɪ	interesting	ɪntrəstɪŋ
apples	æplz	angry	æŋgrɪ
icecreams	aɪskri:mz	next to	neks tə
oranges	ɒrɪndʒɪz		

Unit 28   ɪə (beer)   eə (chair)

Sound production

ɪə   This has two sounds: ɪ and ə. First make the sound ɪ. Then add ə.

eə   This has two sounds: e and ə. First practise the sound e. Then make it a little longer and add ə.

Student difficulties

These sounds are difficult for most students. Although they will be used quite frequently in the words *here, there, their, they're*, at Beginner to Elementary level there are very few other words to practise these sounds.

   As well as the pronunciation of the actual sounds, there is also the problem

of whether the letter 'r' should be pronounced, and it is important for
students to have practised Units 25, 26 and 27 before beginning this unit.

ɪə   Most students pronounce this iːr with the 'r' always pronounced. This
      causes little misunderstanding as native speakers are used to this in a
      Scottish or American accent, but if students are learning Received
      Pronunciation English ɪə should be practised.

eə   Most students pronounce this er with the 'r' always pronounced. Arabic
      speakers may also confuse iː and eə.

Beginners will be using the word *there* frequently, and may be confused
by the different uses of this word and the change in pronunciation in its
unstressed form. Compare:

There's a book on the table.

It's there.

In the first sentence the word 'there' is used to introduce a sentence in which
the subject (a book) follows the verb (is). The word 'there' is unstressed, and
in rapid speech most native speakers would tend to say ðez or ðəz, and
would say ðeəz only when speaking slowly or very correctly. In the second
sentence the word 'there' is an adverb of place, contrasted with 'here'. The
word 'there' is stressed and pronounced ðeə.

Linking up with course work

Link up with practice in asking where people and places are.

   See *Further practice* (below).

Suggested procedures

EXERCISE I

Note: In this exercise the letter 'r' is pronounced only in the words: *aeroplane*,
hairdresser's (second 'r').

   Falling intonation in statements and 'wh' questions. Rising intonation in
the Yes/No questions: 'Is it near here?' and 'Here?' (Is it here?).

Steps

1 Students listen to the tape or teacher reading the words in the comic strip,
   then repeat these.
2 Check understanding of words for substitution.
3 Students practise role playing in pairs.

EXERCISE 2

Note: Words for substitution: book, hat, pen, pencil, pipe, bag.

   Pronunciation of final 'r' in newspaper before vowels.

   Pronunciation of *There's a* ðez ə in A's sentence; in B's sentence: *there* ðeə,
here hɪə. See *Student difficulties*.

Steps
1 Students practise chorally first A's sentences, then B's. Tap with a ruler to show stress timing for both sentences. Although the two written sentences are approximately the same length, A's sentence should be said in a much shorter time as this has only two main stresses.
2 Students practise in pairs as in the Example.

EXERCISE 3

Note: Pronunciation of 'r' before the word 'it' in the last line.

Steps
1 Students listen to the dialogue on tape or read by the teacher.
2 Practise the first and last lines of the dialogue.
3 Students practise the whole dialogue in pairs.

Further practice

Asking where places are. Example:
A: Excuse me. Where's the ★? Is it near here?
B: Yes. It's over there./Sorry. I don't know where it is.
A: Thank you.
★ toilet/way in/way out/cafeteria/staff room/other examples relevant to students' environment.

Asking where people are. Example:
Give students' names as cues.
T: Mr X.
A: Where's Mr X? Is he here?
B: Yes. He's over there.
T: Mr X and Miss Y.
A: Where are Mr X and Miss Y? Are they here?
X and Y: We're here!
B: They're over there!

Spelling

The sound ɪə is usually written with the letters 'ea'.
Examples: dear, ear, hear, near, really.
Other spellings: here, we're

The sound eə is usually written with the letters 'are' or 'ere'.
Examples: careful, square, where, there
Other spellings: their, they're, wear, aeroplane

Pronunciation of some words in this unit

beer	bɪə	**ae**roplane	eərəpleɪn
near	nɪə	**hair**dresser's	heədresəz
here	hɪə	**air**port	eəpɔːt
chair	tʃeə	ex**cuse** me	ekskjuːz miː
where	weə	square	skweə
there	ðeə		

Unit 29 ʊ (book)

Sound production

First practise the sound ɒ. Then put the back of your tongue forward and up a little. ʊ is a very short sound.

Student difficulties

Many students have difficulty in distinguishing the sounds ʊ (foot) and uː (boot). This is particularly difficult for French, Portuguese, Greek, Farsi, Italian and Spanish speakers. Turkish, Chinese and Indo-Chinese speakers may also have some difficulty. In this unit ʊ is contrasted with another short vowel, ɒ. Students should try to make ʊ short, as this will help in distinguishing it from uː. Confusion of these sounds is no doubt increased by spelling as both sounds are often spelt with 'oo' and this looks as though it should be a long sound. It would help students to begin practice of Exercise 1 with the words masked.

Linking up with course work

Link up with teaching and practice of imperatives in describing how to do something, for example: how to start/stop a car. See suggestions in *Further practice*.

Suggested procedures

EXERCISE 1

For suggested teaching procedures for minimal pairs, see page 104.
Contrasts for further practice: pot/put; God/good.

EXERCISE 2

Note: Cookery books = books about how to cook.
Pronunciation of final 'r' in *water*: water is; water in.
Students repeat words on the picture.

EXERCISE 3

Note: Falling intonation.

Steps
1 Practise the two examples tapping with a ruler to establish stress patterns.
2 Students make sentences as in the examples, then repeat the exercise giving answers at the same pace as the stress pattern is tapped out with a ruler.

Further practice

Students make sentences from the blackboard which are appropriate to the teacher's verbal cues:
Blackboard:

	brake	
(Don't) Put your foot on the	accelerator	
	clutch	

Teacher's cues:
I want to start the car/stop the car/change gear/go up a hill/go down a hill/go faster/go slower/overtake another car.
Note: brake breɪk; accelerator əkseləreɪtə; clutch klʌtʃ.

Spelling

The sound ʊ is usually written with the letters 'oo' or 'u'.
Examples:
oo   book, cook, foot, good, look, wood, room (rʊm)
u   full, pull, push, put, sugar

Other spelling: *o*   woman

Pronunciation of some words in this unit

cookery	kʊkərɪ	look	lʊk
sugar	ʃʊgə	push	pʊʃ
woman	wʊmən	pull	pʊl
empty	emptɪ	wood	wʊd

Unit 30   u: (boot)

Sound production

First practise the sound ʊ again. ʊ is a short sound. Then put your tongue up and back. u: is a long sound.

Student difficulties

See notes on student difficulties in Unit 29.

Linking up with course work

Link up with practice in asking what people like.

Suggested procedures

EXERCISE 1

For suggested teaching procedures for minimal pairs, see page 104.
   Contrasts for further practice: full/fool. Stress that sound 2 is a long sound. If students have difficulty in understanding this, write the minimal pair words on the blackboard:
look   Luuuuke
pull   pooool
and students use this to practise the words and sentences.

EXERCISE 2

Note: Words for substitution in column A practise ʊ; column B: u:; column C: ʊ/u:.
   Rising intonation in the Yes/No question.
   Pronunciation of the unstressed words 'do you' in the question: də ju: or in very rapid speech: dju:.

Steps
1 Students listen to the dialogue on tape or read by the teacher, then practise it.
2 Students practise the words for substitution in columns A, B and C. Particularly with column C it will be very helpful to practise from the blackboard first as in Exercise 1:

B	C
muuuusic	good fooood
fruuuuit	bluuuue rooms
schooool	good schooools
bluuuue shooooes	looking at pooools
swimming pooools	looking at the moooon

3 Practice the question with different cues from A, B, C. For example:
   Teacher: football
   Students: Do you like football?
4 Students practise the dialogue with substitutions in pairs.

Further practice

a) Students practise from the blackboard:
    blue suits   looking at new books
    apple juice   good students
    rainy afternoons   wearing wooden shoes
    pop music   wearing football boots
    (suits su:ts; juice dʒu:s; **stu**dents stju:dnts; **woo**den wʊdn;
    boots bu:ts)
b) Conversation in pairs and reporting on likes and dislikes using the
    blackboard material.
    Example:
    Student A: Do you like apple juice?
    Student B: Yes, I do./No, I don't./ I don't mind it (them).
    Student A asks five questions, makes notes on B's answers, then gives a
    report, for example: 'He likes apple juice and pop music. He doesn't
    mind blue suits. He doesn't like wearing wooden shoes or football boots.'

Spelling

The sound u: is usually written with the letters 'u' or 'oo'.
Examples:
u   music, pupil, student, January, February, June
oo afternoon, food, moon, school, soon, spoon, too

Other spellings:
o/oe   do, to, who, whose, lose, move, shoe
ui   fruit, suit
ou   you, group
ew   new, few
others two, through

Pronunciation of some words in this unit

boot   bu:t   **mu**sic   mju:zɪk
Luke   lu:k   good **food**   gʊd fu:d
pull   pʊl   blue **rooms**   blu: rʊmz (*or* ru:mz)
June   dʒu:n   good **schools**   gʊd sku:lz
Sue   su: **loo**king at **pools**   lʊkɪn ət pu:lz
moon   mu:n   **lots** of **su**gar   lɒts əv ʃʊgə

Unit 31   t (tin)

Sound production

Step 1 Put the front of your tongue behind your top teeth. Push air forward in your mouth.
Step 2 Then move your tongue away, releasing the air.
Note: This describes the production of aspirated t, as it is pronounced before a vowel. Compare the sound t in the word 'what' in: *What a fat cat!* (aspirated t) and *What fat cats!* (unaspirated t). In the unaspirated t Step 2 is omitted, making it a quieter sound before a consonant.

Student difficulties

At the end of words Spanish speakers may confuse the sounds t and tʃ, Italian speakers may confuse t and ts. Many students – for example, Greek, Italian, Spanish, Dutch, French and speakers of Slavic languages – tend to use an unaspirated t which to English speakers will often sound like d. Also native English speakers often do not aspirate t in the final position, and many students find this difficult.

Linking up with course work

Link up with teaching of how to express surprise in exclamations, for example: Look at that/Just look at that/What a/Isn't that a pretty telephone!

Suggested procedures

EXERCISE 1

Note: In all examples here t is followed by a vowel and is a loud sound (aspirated t).
  Strongly falling intonation in exclamations of surprise.

Steps: Students listen and repeat words on the pictures, then make exclamations, as in the Examples, using the words *pretty* or *dirty* as appropriate to the picture.

EXERCISE 2

Note: With the exception of *What a*, all examples of the sound t here are unaspirated and should be a quiet sound.
  Many students have difficulty with the final consonant cluster ts in: it's, that's, what's, cats, hats, etc.
  The material in this exercise can be used to give Italian speakers practice in the contrasts: *a fat cat/a fatter cat*; *a wet hat/a wetter hat*. Use blackboard drawings and drill, for example:

Student A: That's a fat cat.

Student B: But that's a fatter cat.

Steps
1 Students listen and repeat singular items first: a fat cat, a wet hat etc.
2 For each item practise the contrasts: a fat cat; fat cats and the exclamations: What a fat cat! What fat cats!
3 Practise the first two lines of the dialogue for several items.
4 Students practise the dialogue in pairs as in the *Example*, making a dialogue for each item.

Further practice

Use a teaching clock to practise: What's the time? It's two/ten/twelve/twenty/eight/sixteen minutes to two/ten/twelve/eight.

Final **ts**: There are lots of	pockets lights students	in those	suits streets boats

Spelling

The sound **t** is written with the letter 't'.
Examples: time, tree, twenty, hat, what, street

Other spellings:
te   plate, late, white, write, minute
tt   better, letter, matter, little
doubling t before 'ing'   sit – sitting; cut – cutting; shut – shutting; put – putting; get – getting
doubling t before 'er'   fat – fatter; hot – hotter; wet – wetter

Pronunciation of some words in this unit

telephone	teləfəʊn	**dir**ty	dɜ:tɪ
toy	tɔɪ	**bis**cuit	bɪskɪt
pretty	prɪtɪ	**qui**et	kwaɪət

Unit 32   d (door)

Sound production

First practise **t**. Use your voice to make **d**.

Student difficulties

Speakers of German, Dutch, Turkish, Spanish, Chinese, Indo-Chinese languages and most Slavic languages have difficulty with this sound, pronouncing it as **t**, particularly at the end of a word. Spanish speakers tend to pronounce **d** close to **ð** in the middle of a word.

Show students that the voice is used for **d** but not **t**.

Linking up with course work

Link up with a) asking what people like;
b) teaching of adjectives (adjectives used in this unit: sad, hard, wide, old, cold, round, red, bad, good).

Suggested procedures

EXERCISE 1

For suggested teaching procedures for minimal pairs, see page 104.

Contrasts for further practice: two/do; town/down; bat/bad; try/dry; Bert/bird.

EXERCISE 2

Note: In the first part of the exercise, students are practising **d** at the end of a word.

For Italian speakers this material can also be used to contrast, for example, *a hard bed/a harder bed* as suggested for Unit 31 Exercise 2.

In the *Sentence practice*:
a) Rising intonation in the questions 'Do you like ...?' and 'Do you?'
b) Weak form of *do* in the questions: **də**.
c) Change in stress and pronunciation in the word 'you' from the unstressed **jə** in 'Do you like ...?' to the stressed **ju:** in 'Do you?'
d) Students may have difficulty with the final consonant cluster **dz** which is being practised here: **bedz**; **bɜ:dz**; **hedz**; **frendz**; **rəʊdz**; **wɪndz**.

Steps
1 Students practise the words listed at the beginning, then complete the phrases for each picture: a hard bed; a sad bird; a round head; an old friend; a wide road; a cold wind.
2 Students practise the dialogue in the Examples.

3 Practise words in note 4 above, then students make dialogues for the other pictures, practising in pairs.

EXERCISE 3

Note: Here students are practising the linking of **d** sounds between words, for example: a bad dog.

Steps

1 Students practise the list of words at the beginning of this exercise.
2 Show on the blackboard how **d** sounds are linked between words, for example: a good dog, a red door, an old dress.
3 Students choose and read the correct answers for each item: a bad dog; a cold day; a wide desk; a good doctor; an old door; a red dress.

Further practice

Pair practice for **t** and **d**:

A: What would you like to do	tonight?
	tomorrow night?
	on Saturday night?

B: I'd like to	go to bed early.
	read a good book.
	eat delicious food in a restaurant.
	watch a good show on TV.
	go dancing with an old friend.
	listen to the radio.

Spelling

The sound **d** is written with the letter 'd'.
Examples: dog, dress, hand, bed, old, under

Other spellings:
de   beside, side, wide, ride
dd   address, midday

Pronunciation of some words in this unit

dead   **ded**
ride   **raɪd**
card   **kɑːd**
hard   **hɑːd**
wide   **waɪd**

Unit 33 aʊ (house)

Sound production

This has two sounds. First practise the sound **æ**. Then add **ʊ**. The second sound is a very short sound.

Student difficulties

Many students have little difficulty with this sound. The most common error is to omit the second part of the diphthong, thus confusing it with **æ**, or to make the first part of the diphthong too short. Lao, Vietnamese, and – to a lesser extent – Khmer speakers tend to drop any final consonant after a diphthong.

Linking up with course work

Link up with a) practice of questions beginning with the word 'how', for example, asking: how people get to work and how long it takes; how far away places are; how much things cost;

b) teaching of questions for countables and uncountables: How many . . . ?/How much . . . ?

Suggested procedures

EXERCISE 1

For suggested teaching procedures for minimal pairs, see page 104.

EXERCISE 2

Note: Pronunciation of the letter 'r' in 'there are a'.
    Questions beginning with *How*? have the same falling intonation as 'wh' questions.

Steps
1 Students repeat the words in the picture and the sentences below it.
2 Practise the falling intonation in Student A's question, using the words for substitution.
3 Students practise in pairs as in the *Example*.

Further practice

Students practise asking the teacher questions beginning:
    How far is it from your house to ....?
    How long does it take to get to .... by car?

Write these questions on the blackboard and encourage students to ask them using familiar place names. Reply 'About 2 kilometres', 'About an hour', etc. Then have a student answer the questions.

Spelling

The sound aʊ is written with the letters 'ou' or 'ow'.
Examples:
ou   about, mouth, out, south, count, round
ow   cow, crowd, down, now, town, brown

Pronunciation of some words in this unit

flower(s)	flaʊə(z)	There are a	ðer ər ə
mouse	maʊs	**cows are** there	kaʊz ɑ: ðeə
mice	maɪs	There are **three**	ðer ə θri:
thousand	θaʊznd	**pairs** of **trou**sers	peəz əv traʊzəz

Unit 34   əʊ (phone)

Sound production

This has two sounds ə and ʊ. First practise ə; them make it longer. Add ʊ; this is very short. The first part of this diphthong is very close to ɜ:.

Student difficulties

Nearly all students have difficulty with this sound. Many students' pronunciation of it is close to the Scottish pronunciation of this sound, and this is noticeable as an accent but is usually understandable to native speakers. Most students confuse this sound with ɒ or ɔ:. Begin with some review practice of words from Unit 23 Exercises 1 and 2 to make students aware that the first element in this diphthong is close to the sound ɜ:. Stressing the change in lip position in pronouncing the two elements in this diphthong is usually very helpful. Have students begin by making a sad expression with the lips spread and the corners of the mouth turned down for ɜ:. Then show how the lips are gradually rounded as the tongue gradually rises to make ʊ.

Linking up with course work

Link up with practice in asking people where they are going and replying to this (Present or Future meaning).

Suggested procedures

EXERCISE 1

For suggested teaching procedures for minimal pairs, see page 104.
    Contrasts for further practice:
ɜ:/əʊ   sir/so; work/woke; girl/goal; curled/cold; learn/loan
ɔ:/əʊ   ball/bowl; called/cold; cork/coke; call/coal; chalk/choke

EXERCISE 2

Note: Falling intonation in exclamation of surprise, 'Oh!'.

Steps. Students:
1 listen and repeat the words and sentences accompanying the picture at the beginning of this exercise;
2 listen to the dialogue on tape or read by the teacher;
3 listen and repeat dialogue and phrases for substitution;
4 practise the dialogue in pairs.

Further practice

Practice of the question 'Where are you going?' with Future meaning:
A: **Where** are you **go**ing to**mor**row?
B: ★ .... **Where** are **you** going?
A: ★ ....
★ I'm going bowling. / I'm going boating. / Nowhere. I'm staying at home. /
I don't know.

Spelling

The sound əʊ is usually written with the letters 'o', 'oa', or 'ow'.
Examples:
o   go, hello, no, old, only, hotel
o . . . e   home, hole, pole, nose, telephone, those
oa   boat, coat, road, Joan
ow   know, low, narrow, show, slow, throw, tomorrow, window, yellow

Other spellings: Oh, sew, toe

Pronunciation of some words in this unit

Bert	bɜːt	he**llo**	heləʊ
Boat	bəʊt	Joan	dʒəʊn
Pearl	pɜːl	Paul	pɔːl
pole	pəʊl	**Jone**s's	dʒəʊnzɪz
saw	sɔː	**gro**cer's	grəʊsəz
sew	səʊ	hotel	həʊtel
corner	kɔːnə	**bow**ling alley	bəʊlɪŋ ælɪ

Unit 35   s/linking s

Note: This unit:
a) provides practice in linking **s**;
b) re-practises the sound **s** in preparation for the following units on ʃ and tʃ.

Sound production

See notes on Units 1 and 2.

Student difficulties

Many students have difficulty in linking **s** sounds between words. Linking of these sounds occurs frequently at beginner level as these sounds occur at the ends of words not only in the plural of nouns, but also in many key structure words, for example: *is, it's, this*.

Note: **z** at the end of a word becomes **s** when the next word begins with 's' or 'sh'. *Example*:
Whose is it?   huːz ɪz ɪt
Whose seat is it?   huː(s)siːt ɪz ɪt
This applies to key words such as: *these, those, whose, who's, his*.

Linking up with course work

Link up with describing actions in the Present Continuous tense using 3rd person singular. Linking **s** will occur when the verb begins with 's', for example: He's studying English. She's sleeping. See Exercise 2.

Suggested procedures

EXERCISE 1

Steps. Students:
1 listen and repeat the words and phrases under the pictures. If students have particular difficulty in joining **s** sounds, practise some examples from the blackboard first:
thisssseat; thissssuit; thisssstick, etc.
Back-chaining is also very helpful, for example:
iːt; siːt; ɪsiːt; ðɪsiːt.
2 make questions and answers in pairs as in the *Example*. B's answer can be negative: 'No. It isn't a very nice seat.'

EXERCISE 2

Note: *'s* is pronounced:
s following unvoiced consonants, for example: *Luke's, Janet's, Pat's*.

z following voiced consonants and vowels, for example: *Paul's, Ted's, Sue's, Sam's, who's*. (But see note under *Student difficulties*.)

Linking of s sounds in bus stop.

Steps

1 Students listen and repeat the following looking at the pictures: 1. Luke. Luke's studying.   2. Janet. Janet's sewing.   3. Pat. Pat's saying Hello.   4. Paul. Paul's stopping a bus.   5. Ted. Ted's sleeping.   6. Sue. Sue's swimming.

Practise examples from blackboard as suggested in Exercise 1 if students have difficulty in linking sounds.

2 Students practise the answers to questions made from the list of substitutions, for example: T: Who's smiling?   S: Sue's smiling. Students may be able to give several answers to some of these questions.

3 Students practise in pairs as in the *Example*.

Further practice

If appropriate, make a list of students' names on the blackboard. Practise sentences with these, for example: Mr Lee's studying English. Miss Tripp's studying English.

Students all change seats at random. Then practise:

Teacher: Miss A. Mr B.

Miss A: Whose seat are you in?

Mr. B: Mr Y's seat.

Miss A: Who's sitting in your seat?

Mr. B: Miss Z's sitting in my seat.

Have the two questions written on the blackboard as prompts.

Pronunciation of some words in this unit

suit	suːt	Paul's	pɔːlz
supper	sʌpə	Ted's	tedz
Sam's	sæmz	Sue's	suːz
Luke's	luːks	who's	huːz
Janet's	dʒænɪts	Pat's	pæts

Unit 36 ∫ (shoe)

Sound production

First practise **s**. Then put your tongue up and back a little to make ∫.

Student difficulties

The sounds **s** and ∫ are confused by Spanish, Dutch and, particularly, Greek speakers. Portuguese and Chinese speakers may also have some difficulty with this sound. Speakers of Spanish, Lao and Vietnamese may confuse ∫ and t∫. Japanese and Chinese speakers may tend to confuse ∫ and **h** at the beginning of words before the sounds iː or ɪ, and this will be particularly noticeable in distinguishing the words 'he' and 'she'. For students who find ∫ a very difficult sound, spend some time on the mouth position and practising the sound in isolation.

Linking up with course work

Link up with practice in asking and talking about nationality.

Suggested procedures

EXERCISE 1

For suggested teaching procedures for minimal pairs, see page 104.
    Contrasts for further practice: sort/short; sew/show; sell/shell; suit/shoot.
Note: The first sentence in (a) may be heard in conversation, but it is more correct to say 'the sea'.

EXERCISE 2

Note: Linking of **z** and ∫ sounds in 'is she'. This is usually pronounced ɪ∫iː. (See note on *Student difficulties* in Unit 35.)
    Intonation in questions with *or*: rising intonation before the word or, falling intonation at the end.
    Pronunciation of *French*: frent∫ or fren∫.

Steps
1 *Example*: Picture 1.
   Teacher: She comes from England. Is she Scottish or English?
   Student(s): She's English.
2 *Example*: Picture 1.
   Teacher: Is she Scottish?
   Student(s): No, she isn't. She's English.
3 Students practise the questions, e.g. Is she Scottish? Is she Scottish or English? with particular attention to intonation in these.
4 Students practise in pairs as in the *Examples*.

Further practice

a) Ask questions about nationality of female students in the class – or of
    women known to the class.
    Examples:
    Teacher: Is Miss X Irish or Scottish?
    Student(s): She isn't Irish *or* Scottish! She's Swedish.
    Teacher: Is Mrs Y from Turkey?
    Student(s): Yes. She's Turkish.

b) Using students' suggestions make a list of famous people of each
    nationality mentioned in this unit. Then practise questions and answer:
    What nationality is X? He's/She's ....
    Examples: Margaret Thatcher (English); James Joyce (Irish); James Watt,
    Sir Walter Scott (Scottish); Alfred Nobel (Swedish); Hans Christian
    Anderson (Danish); General de Gaulle (French); General Franco
    (Spanish); Kemal Ataturk (Turkish); Leonid Brezhnev, V. Lenin
    (Russian); Jean Sibelius (Finnish).

Spelling

The sound ʃ is written with the letters 'sh'.
Examples: fish, ship, shop, push, sunshine, finish
Other spellings: Russia, Russian, sugar

Pronunciation of some words in this unit

Scottish	skɒtıʃ	Spain	speın
Ireland	aıələnd	**Spa**nish	spænıʃ
Irish	aıərıʃ	**Ru**ssia	rʌʃə
Sweden	swi:dn	**Ru**ssian	rʌʃn
Swedish	swi:dıʃ	**Fin**nish	fınıʃ
Danish	deınıʃ	**Tur**key	tɜ:kı
Polish	pəʊlıʃ	**Tur**kish	tɜ:kıʃ
French	frentʃ		

Unit 37 ʒ (television)

Sound production

First practise ʃ. Use your voice to make ʒ.

Student difficulties

Many students find this sound difficult, particularly Dutch, German,

Scandinavian, Greek, Italian, Spanish, Lao, Khmer, Chinese and Japanese speakers. Arabic speakers may also have some difficulty with this sound. This sound is replaced by sounds close to ʃ or z or dʒ. However, at beginner level there are very few words that students will learn with this sound.

Linking up with course work

Link up with talking about what people do every day using the word 'usually'.

Suggested procedures

If necessary, check students' understanding of the Present Simple tense and the word 'usually' (nearly always, nearly every day) using the list of days of the week at the beginning of this exercise.

Steps
1 Students listen and repeat or make sentences using the word 'usually' for each picture.
   Picture 1 : Sue usually wakes up at seven o'clock.
2 Students practise questions and answers in pairs as in the *Example*.

Further practice

Practise questions and answers about the students' own daily routine using the pictures as prompts, for example: Picture 1. What time do you usually get up? I usually get up at ....

Spelling

The sound ʒ is usually written with the letters 's' or 'ge'.
Examples:
s   usually, unusual, Asia, measure, pleasure, television
ge garage

Pronunciation of some words in this unit

| lunch | lʌntʃ | o'**clock** | əklɒk |
| **break**fast | brekfəst | **u**sually | juːʒli |

Unit 38 tʃ (cherry)

Sound production

First practise t and ʃ. Begin to make t. Then slowly move your tongue from the roof of your mouth.

Student difficulties

Portuguese, French, Chinese, Dutch, Scandinavian and Greek speakers have difficulty with this sound. A very common error is to confuse it with ʃ. Greek students may pronounce it ts and Danes tj. Speakers of Indo-Chinese languages have some difficulty with this sound at the end of words: Lao and Khmer speakers may confuse it with t and some Vietnamese speakers may confuse it with ʃ.

Linking up with course work

Link up with:
a) teaching of countables and uncountables and with practice in asking about and describing quantities using the expressions *how much/too much*;
b) practice in asking how much things cost.

Suggested procedures

EXERCISE 1

For suggested teaching procedures for minimal pairs, see page 104.
    Contrasts for further practice: ship/chip; shop/chop; shoe/chew; wish/which.

EXERCISE 2

Note: Examples of countables in this exercise: chair, picture, watch, match, bottle of sherry. The classification of uncountables is more debatable. Cakes, pies, chickens and fish can of course be counted. But here it is best to classify them as uncountables as they are being considered as quantities of food, and for this reason are shown in the illustration as incomplete, for example: not a whole cake but a quantity of cake.
    Weak form of *some* səm.
    Joining of z and s sounds in 'there'ş some'.

Steps
1 Students listen and repeat words in the illustration.
2 Make sentences as in Examples A (countables) and B (uncountables). See Note above.

EXERCISE 3

Note: Unlike other fricatives, the sounds tʃ and dʒ are not joined between words; both sounds are pronounced separately.

Falling intonation as in 'wh' questions for questions beginning with the word 'how'.

Weak forms: *there's* ðəz, *for* fə.

Steps

1 Practise the question, paying particular attention to intonation and the separate pronunciation of tʃ and ʃ sounds in How much cheese/chicken/cherry pie/chocolate cake/chinese food/sherry/sugar is there?
2 Practise some examples of the answers, changing the number – one child, twenty children, etc. – to check the students' understanding of meaning.
3 Students practise in pairs as in the *Example*.

Further practice

Students look at the food in the illustration for Exercise 2. Imagine these are in a restaurant or canteen. Choose an item and ask the cost, for example:
'How much is a portion of chicken?'
'How much does a portion of chicken cost?'
The teacher or another student should give answers to the questions.

Spelling

The sound tʃ is usually written with the letters 'ch'.
Examples: cheap, child, church, rich, teacher, which

Other spellings:
tch   kitchen, match, watch, butcher
t   picture, question

Pronunciation of some words in this unit

cherry	tʃerɪ	pie	paɪ
lunch	lʌntʃ	**kit**chen	kɪtʃɪn
chocolate	tʃɒklət	match	mætʃ
picture	pɪktʃə	chalk	tʃɔːk
children	tʃɪldrn	**chi**cken	tʃɪkɪn
e**nough**	ɪnʌf		

Unit 39   dʒ (jam)

Sound production

First practise tʃ. Use your voice to make dʒ.

Student difficulties

Many students have difficulty with this sound. Portuguese, Arabic, French and Vietnamese speakers may pronounce it ʒ, Danes dj, and Greeks dz. Spanish speakers may confuse j and dʒ. German, Dutch, Turkish and Chinese speakers may confuse it with tʃ.

Linking up with course work

Link up with practice in asking questions beginning with 'which'.

Suggested procedures

EXERCISE I

For suggested teaching procedures for minimal pairs, see page 104.
     Contrasts for further practice: H/age; larch/large; chain/Jane; chess/Jess; chin/gin. It may be helpful to contrast the sounds d and dʒ as well. *Examples*: day/Jay; dust/just; dam/jam; deep/jeep; door/jaw.

EXERCISE 2

Note: Falling intonation in 'wh' questions.
     Pronunciation of 'r' in *a jar of jam*.
     Fridge frɪdʒ, (plural) *fridges* frɪdʒɪz: short for *refrigerator*.
     In pair practice work students should make the question plural: 'Which fridge are the oranges/vegetables in?'

Steps
1 Students practise the questions and words in the first illustration of the two fridges. It may be helpful to divide the sounds tʃ and dʒ in initial practice:
     tʃ   chicken, cheese, cherry pie, chocolate cake
     dʒ   cabbage, Japanese food, German sausage, orange juice, oranges, jelly,
       a jar of jam
2 Students practise in pairs as in the *Example*. There is constant repetition of the sound ɪ here, and this is a good opportunity to check students' pronunciation of this sound.

EXERCISE 3

Note: This exercise provides an opportunity for review practice in the following sounds:
s   centre, shops, writes, entrance, rest, largest
z   his, Joe's, letters
ʃ   shopping, shop
tʃ   butcher, each, cheapest
dʒ   Joe, Joe's, large, largest

Steps
1 Introduce any new vocabulary, for example: *butcher, shopping centre, each, main entrance, next to each other.*
2 Students listen to the joke on tape or read by the teacher.
3 If you wish to use this material for a review of fricatives, write (or collect from the joke with students' help) words on the blackboard as in the note above and practise from this.
4 Students read the joke aloud in pairs or groups.

Further practice

Using the illustrations in their book, each student writes and asks a question, for example:
Student: On which page is there a picture of a zoo?
Teacher: Page 10.
Student: No. Page 6.
The number of pages could be limited, e.g. illustrations from Units 1–10 only, and students could make a team game of this question.

Spelling

The sound dʒ is usually written with the letters 'j' or 'ge'.
Examples:
j   job, jump, joke, January, June, July, jeep
ge   age, large, orange, vegetable, sausage, cabbage
g   German, gentleman
dge bridge, fridge

Pronunciation of some words in this unit

choke	tʃəʊk	Japan**ese**	dʒæpəniːz
joke	dʒəʊk	ca**bb**age	kæbɪdʒ
fridge	frɪdʒ	**ve**getable	vedʒtəbl
German	dʒɜːmən	**or**anges	ɒrɪndʒɪz
sausage	sɒsɪdʒ	a **jar** of **jam**	ə dʒɑːr əv dʒæm
large	lɑːdʒ	**cho**colate	tʃɒklət

Unit 40 j (yellow)

Sound production

First practise i:. *Very quickly* move your tongue to make the next sound. Do *not* touch the roof of your mouth with your tongue.

Student difficulties

This sound is pronounced close to dʒ by Spanish and some German speakers. Some Portuguese speakers may tend to omit it. This sound is also difficult for Chinese and Japanese speakers before the sounds i: or ɪ. Although this sound is used frequently by beginners in the words 'yes' and 'you', there are few other words for practice at this level.

Show students that the tongue position for this sound is initially the same as i:. Begin with practice of some words with this sound, for example: E, eat, easy. Some of students' confusion over the sound j is caused by spelling, and the phonetic symbol does not help. If necessary practise some words from the first column in Exercise 1 on the blackboard, thus:
Write *you*, then rub out the letter 'y' and replace it with EE or i:: EEou, EEes, etc.

Linking up with course work

Link up with
a) formal introductions,
b) making and replying to compliments.

Suggested procedures

EXERCISE 1

See suggestion under *Student difficulties* above.

If necessary, explain the greeting: 'Happy New Year'. Ask: 'Which day of the year do people say 'Happy New Year'?'

EXERCISE 2

Steps
1 Students listen to the conversations on tape or read by the teacher. Books open.
2 Books closed. Students listen again. Stop the tape after the first person in each conversation has spoken. Students try to remember what the second person said.
3 Students practise reading the conversations in pairs.

Further practice

Introductions Example:
Student A: Mr. B, this is Mr. C.
         Mr. C, I'd like you to meet Mr. B.
Student B: How do you do?
Student C: How do you do?
(Note falling intonation in this question.)

Compliments Example:
Student A: I like your ★.............................
         Your ★............................. is (are) very nice.
Student B: Thank you.
★ hat, bag, tie, dress, coat, skirt, shirt, socks, shoes, trousers, glasses.
(Note rising intonation in the compliment.)

Spelling

The sound j is usually written with the letters 'y' or 'u'.
Examples:
y   yes, you, yellow, year, young, yesterday
u   music, student, pupil, January, usually

Other spelling: new

Pronunciation of some words in this unit

yellow	jeləʊ	**J**anuary	dʒænjʊərɪ
year	jɜ:	**stu**dent	stju:dnt
new	nju:	Portu**guese**	pɔ:tʃʊgi:z
music	mju:zɪk	pro**nounce**	prənɑʊns
How do you **do**	haʊ də ju: du:		

Unit 41   eɪ (tail)

Sound production

This has two sounds: e and ɪ. First make the sound e. Make it longer. Then add ɪ. This second sound is very short.

Student difficulties

Arabic, French, Italian, Greek, Japanese, Lao, Portuguese, German, Hebrew, Scandinavian, Chinese and Turkish speakers have some difficulty. A very common error is to confuse it with **e**. Some students, for example Italian and Greek speakers, may confuse **eɪ** and **aɪ**. Scandinavians make the **ɪ** element in this diphthong too long. Lao, Vietnamese, and – to a lesser extent – Khmer speakers tend to drop any final consonant after a diphthong, and Chinese speakers find this diphthong harder before final consonants. It is usually very helpful to emphasise the gradual change in lip position in making this diphthong.

Linking up with course work

Link up with practice of questions beginning with 'What's' (Present Continuous tense).

Suggested procedures

EXERCISE I

For suggested teaching procedures for minimal pairs, see page 104. Contrasts for further practice:

e/eɪ   get/gate; wet/wait; tell/tail; L/ale; test/taste; letter/later
aɪ/eɪ   I/A; my/may; why/way; like/lake; die/day; bike/bake

EXERCISE 2

Note: Item 6. The letters 'a', 'j' and 'k' have the sound **eɪ**. Ask the students which other letter has the same sound (h).

Item 7. We usually say, 'The eighth of May'. Other examples for practice of **eɪ**: 18 April, 28 May.

Steps
1 Students repeat words in the picture and sentences below.
2 Students read and answer the questions in pair work.

Further practice

Write the following on the blackboard. Students complete it and practise reading:
A **grey** old **lady** from **Spain**
Was af**raid** to fly on a ....
But she **went** up one **day**
And she **said**: 'It's O............................
It's **better** than **go**ing by ....!'
(**plane, K, train**)

Spelling

The sound eɪ is usually written with the letters 'a', 'ay' or 'ai'.
Examples:
a   baby, face, late, page, place, same, take
ay   day, say, stay, today, way
ai   rain, Spain, train, wait

Other spelling: grey, they, break, eight

Pronunciation of some words in this unit

pepper pepə   **ra**dio reɪdɪəʊ
paper peɪpə   James dʒeɪmz
sail seɪl   Fay feɪ
pain peɪn   **rail**way reɪlweɪ
grey greɪ   **sta**tion steɪʃn
aeroplane eərəpleɪn   **news**paper nju:speɪpə
date deɪt

Unit 42 ɔɪ (boy)

Sound production

This has two sounds: ɔ: and ɪ. First say ɔ:. Make it longer. Then add ɪ; this
second sound is very short.

Student difficulties

French speakers tend to drop the second part of the diphthong, and
Scandinavians and Dutch speakers may make the second part too long.
Some students, for example Farsi speakers, may confuse ɔɪ with aɪ. Lao,
Vietnamese, and to a lesser extent Khmer speakers tend to drop any final
consonant after a diphthong. ɔɪ followed by l is the hardest combination of
this sound for many students. There are few words for practice of this sound
at beginner level.

Suggested procedures

Students:
1 practise words and sentences accompanying the illustration;
2 make sentences as in the *Example*: toy train/railway/gate/aeroplane/station
   (*not* newspaper).

Spelling

The sound ɔɪ is written with the letters 'oi' or 'oy'.
Examples:
oi   noise, oil
oy   boy, toy

Pronunciation of some words in this unit

noise   nɔɪz
noisy   nɔɪzɪ

Unit 43   aɪ (fine)

Sound production

This has two sounds: ɑː and ɪ. First practise ɑː; this is a long sound. Then add ɪ; this is a short sound.

Student difficulties

Most students have little difficulty with this sound. Scandinavians may make the second part of the diphthong too long, and French speakers tend to drop the second part of the diphthong. Farsi speakers tend to confuse this sound with ɔɪ. Italian and Greek speakers may confuse it with e. Lao, Vietnamese, and – to a lesser extent – Khmer, speakers tend to drop any final consonant after a diphthong.

Linking up with course work

Link up with
a) practice in saying what you like/don't like;
b) talking about the future using the Present Continuous tense.

Suggested procedures

EXERCISE I

For suggested teaching procedures for minimal pairs see page 104. Contrast for further practice: Ma/my; tar/tie; bar/buy.
For students who confuse aɪ with ɔɪ, first practise: boy/buy; toy/tie; good boy/goodbye.
For students who confuse aɪ and eɪ, practise: A/I; lake/like; late/light; May/my; tray/try; wait/white; bake/bike.

EXERCISE 2

Note: In Section A the sound **aɪ** is followed by a voiced consonant (or silence), and the first part of the diphthong should be a relatively long sound. Students may make the sound **ɑ:** too short here.

In Section B the sound **aɪ** is followed by an unvoiced consonant and the first part of the diphthong should be a shorter sound than in the examples in Section A.

Steps: Students practise words on the pictures and then make sentences (as in the *Examples*) using phrases from both sections.

EXERCISE 3

Note: Here the Present Continuous tense is used for future actions. If students have not already practised this, make sure that they understand that the dialogue is about the future.

Falling intonation in 'Have a nice time!'. This polite expression is frequently used. Other examples: Have a nice day/trip/holiday/weekend/evening.

Steps. Students:
1 listen to the dialogue on tape or read by the teacher;
2 listen and repeat the dialogue and words for substitution;
3 practise in pairs.

Further practice

Use the following blackboard cues to prompt students to practise conversations about future actions: today/at the weekend/in the holidays/this evening.
Example:
Student A: What are you doing at the weekend?
Student B: I'm staying at home.
Student A: Have a nice weekend!
Student B: Thank you.

Spelling

The sound **aɪ** is usually written with the letters 'i' or 'y'.
Examples:
i   I, child, find, Friday, five, smile, time
y   my, fly, cry, sky, dry
igh   high, light, night, right, bright
ye   eye, goodbye
ie   lie, tie
uy   buy

Pronunciation of some words in this unit

Pa	pɑː	rice	raɪs
pie	paɪ	bright	braɪt
cart	kɑːt	**ice**-skating	aɪs skeɪtɪŋ
kite	kaɪt	**ice**-cream	aɪs kriːm
climbing	klaɪmɪŋ	good**night**	gʊdnaɪt
riding	raɪdɪŋ	**Fri**day	fraɪdɪ

Unit 44   p (pen)   b (baby)

Sound production

p   Close your lips hard. Push air forward in your mouth. Then open your
lips quickly. Do not use your voice.

b   First practise p. Use your voice to make b.
Notes on aspiration of t (see Unit 31) also apply to these sounds.

Student difficulties

p   Arabic and Vietnamese speakers tend to pronounce it b, speakers of
some Asian languages and Hebrew may confuse f and p. Speakers of
Italian, Spanish, Greek, French, Dutch, Japanese and Slavic languages
may fail to aspirate this sound, causing confusion with b.

b   Spanish and Portuguese speakers may pronounce this close to v in some
positions. At the end of words the following may pronounce this p:
German, Turkish, Chinese, Indo-Chinese, some Slavic and Spanish
speakers.

Linking up with course work

Link up with practice in asking and saying what somebody's job is.

Suggested procedures

EXERCISE I

For suggested teaching procedures for minimal pairs, see page 104. This
exercise gives practice in p/b contrasts at the beginning of words. Exercise 3
gives practice in p/b contrasts at the ends of words.
Contrasts for further practice: pig/big; penny/Benny; pull/bull; pack/back;
pie/buy.

For students who confuse p with f: foot/put; full/pull; fast/past;
fence/pence; coffee/copy.

EXERCISE 2

Note: Examples in the following sections provide practice in:
A   p at the beginning of words;
B   final p;
C   b at the beginning of words.
Steps. Students listen and repeat.

EXERCISE 3

There are few words at this level to give practice in this contrast.

EXERCISE 4

Students practise words and sentences at the beginning of this exercise, then question and answer for each picture as in the *Example*.

EXERCISE 5

Note: Intonation for items in a list: rising intonation on each item, falling intonation on the last item.

Steps: Each student participating in the game adds a new item to the list, as in the *Example*. The game ends when the list becomes too long for students to remember it.

Further practice

Students practise the following from the blackboard, then use these to play the game described in *Exercise 5*:

a baby's bottle	a book of stamps
a ping-pong ball	a paper boat
a double bed	some Spanish bread
some football boots	a pretty bird
a big cup	a blue plate
a black sheep	a box of pencils

Spelling

The sound p is written with the letter 'p'.
Examples: paper, people, pupil, shop, help
pp happy, supper
doubling p shop – shopping; stop – stopping

The sound b is written with the letter 'b'.
Examples: big, baby, about, bring, number

Pronunciation of some words in this unit

pear peə   potatoes pəteɪtəʊz
butcher bʊtʃə   **cab** driver kæb draɪvə
bear beə   envelope envələʊp
barman bɑːmən   pipe paɪp
picture pɪktʃə   bought bɔːt
Paris pærɪs   some **bread** and **butter**   səm bred ən bʌtə
footballer fʊtbɔːlə   a **bottle** of **beer**   ə bɒtl əv bɪə

Unit 45   k (key)   g (girl)

Sound production

k   Touch the back of the roof of your mouth with the back of your tongue. Push air forward in your mouth. Then move your tongue away.

g   First practise k. Use your voice to make g.
    Notes on aspiration of t (see Unit 31) also apply to these sounds.

Student difficulties

k   Few students have difficulty with this sound. Greek and Turkish speakers may have some difficulty particularly before the sounds iː or ɪ.

g   At the end of words German, Dutch, Turkish, Chinese and speakers of some Slavic languages pronounce this k, and Japanese speakers may also have some difficulty. Indo-Chinese and some Arabic speakers find this sound difficult in all positions.

Linking up with course work

Link up with
a) teaching of adverbs; (Adverbs used here: carefully, quickly, quietly.)
b) practice in telling someone how to do something, for example: Carry the cups. Be careful./Carry the cups carefully.

Suggested procedures

EXERCISE I

For suggested teaching procedures for minimal pairs, see page 104.
    This gives practice in the k/g contrast at the beginning of words. Greek speakers should practise sound 2 first: glass/class, etc. Contrasts for further practice: cot/got; cold/gold; crow/grow; come/gum; carry/Garry.

EXERCISE 2

Steps

1 Students practise words and sentences at the beginning of this exercise. Each pair of sentences has four main stresses. Tap with a ruler to show this stress pattern as students read or repeat the sentences.
2 Practise the sentences using adverbs – *carefully*, *quietly*, *quickly* – as in the *Example*. The second sentence has three main stresses.
3 Students practise in pairs as in the *Example*.

EXERCISE 3

This gives practice in the k/g contrast at the end of words. Note that two sounds are contrasted in Dick's **dɪks** and digs **dɪgz**. Other examples: lock/log; frock/frog; pick/pig; peck/peg; dock/dog.

EXERCISE 4

This gives practice in the sound g at the end of words, and in the final clusters ks and gz, which many students find difficult.

Further practice

Joining k and g sounds between words. Practise the following from the blackboard, then students practise in pairs: question and answer – reporting of answers.

k k   Do you like: cooking/questions/cold coffee/careful drivers/crowded places/quiet girls/clean kitchens/cutting cakes?

k g   Do you like: games/guns/gardening/getting presents/giving presents/ going to parties/green gloves/grey skies?

g g   Do you like big: girls/gardens/guns/gloves/goats/glasses/green frogs/ grey snakes?

g k   Do you like big: classes/crowds/keys/clocks/kitchens/cups/coats/cows?

Spelling

The sound k is written with the letters 'k', 'c', 'ck', 'qu' or 'x'.
Examples:
k   kind, ask, drink, sky, speak, dark
ke   like, make, take
ck   back, black, pocket, thick, truck, clock, chicken
c   can, come, cold, copy, doctor, music
qu   (pronounced kw) quarter, question, quick, quiet, square
x   (pronounced ks) box, next, six, taxi
Other spelling: school

The sound g is written with the letter 'g'.
Examples: go, get, grass, begin, bag, again
gg   egg
doubling g   big – bigger; fog – foggy

Pronunciation of some words in this unit

curl	kɜːl	dogs	dɒgz
girl	gɜːl	eggs	egz
quietly	kwaɪətlɪ	cakes	keɪks
quickly	kwɪklɪ	figs	fɪgz
carefully	keəflɪ	frogs	frɒgz
coffee	kɒfɪ	clocks	klɒks

Unit 46   s (sun)   z (zoo)

Note: This unit:
a)   gives practise in final consonant clusters ending in s or z;
b)   reviews consonant clusters practised in Units 24, 31, 32 and 45.

Sound production

See Units 1 and 2.

Student difficulties

The final consonant clusters practised in this Unit are difficult for many
students. At beginner level these clusters ending in s or z occur mainly in the
words 'it's', 'what's' and 'that's' and the plurals of nouns, which were
practised in Units 1 and 2. Using the Simple Present tense, elementary
students have not only the problem of remembering to add s or z to the
third person singular, but also the difficulty of final consonant clusters with
many of these words.
    The letter 's' added to the third person singular is pronounced:
s   after unvoiced consonants: p/t/k/f/θ. *Examples*: stops, eats, cooks.
z   after vowels or voiced consonants: b/d/g/v/l/n/m/ŋ/ð. *Examples*: plays,
    rides, digs, sings.
(But see note under *Student difficulties* in Unit 35.)
    The letters 'es' (pronounced ɪz or əz) are added after fricatives
s/z/ʃ/tʃ/dʒ/ʒ. *Examples*: washes, watches.
    The two exercises in this unit provide, for elementary students, quite
extensive practice and, particularly with a weak to average class, it would be
best to teach them in two separate lessons.

Linking up with course work

Link up with talking about what work different people do.

Suggested procedures

EXERCISE I

Note: Words in the first two columns below the illustrations all end in the sound **s**. Words in the third column end in **s** or **z**.
The sounds **w**, **ð** and **θ** are repeated frequently in practising this exercise.

Steps
1 Check that students understand that the Simple Present tense is being used here. *Example*: The first man makes clocks on Monday/Tuesday, etc./every day.
2 Check ordinal numbers with questions and short answers on pictures 1–12:
   Teacher: Which man makes clocks – the first man or the second man?
   Student: The first man.
3 Students listen and repeat words in the first two columns and the sentence in the *Example*: writes books; The third man writes books.
4 Students listen and repeat the question in the *Example*. Check falling intonation. Then practise, for example:
   Teacher: writes books.
   Student A: Which man writes books?
   Student B: The first man writes books.
5 Repeat steps 3–4 above for words in column 3.
6 Students practise alone in pairs.

EXERCISE 2

Note: Words in the first column after the illustrations end in **s** or **z**. Words in column 2 all end in **z** and words in column 3 end in **z** or **əz**. Note pronunciation of clothes **kləʊðz**, which even native speakers find difficult and sometimes pronounce **kləʊz**.
   Students of some cultural backgrounds may have difficulty in understanding even the first three of the titles at the beginning of this exercise. Check that students can pronounce these and that they understand that they are used only with surnames: Mr **mɪstə** for men; Mrs **mɪsɪz** for married women; Miss **mɪs** for unmarried women; Ms **mɪz** or **məz** a new title for women. Check pronunciation of the **s**/**z** contrast in **mɪs**/**mɪz**.

Steps
1 Check that students understand that the actions described happen regularly/every day, i.e. Simple Present tense.

2 Students practise the titles at the beginning of the exercise.
3 Students listen and repeat or read the name on each picture. This exercise reviews many names introduced in previous units.
4 As for Steps 3–6 in Exercise 1, following the *Example* in this exercise.

Further practice

Other words at this level with final consonant clusters ending in z.
Underlined words in this list have three or more consonants in the cluster.

bz   Bob's, jobs, cabs, pubs
dz   beds, birds, crowds, roads, sides, woods, needs, rides, <u>holds</u>, <u>finds</u>, <u>sends</u>, <u>stands</u>, <u>hands</u>, <u>friends</u>, <u>husbands</u>, <u>seconds</u>
gz   bags, eggs, legs
vz   lives, wives, knives, loaves, leaves
mz   arms, farms, games, homes, names, rooms, times, comes, swims
nz   aeroplanes, guns, kitchens, pens, questions, sons, spoons, telephones, towns, trains, begins, cleans, learns, opens, runs, shines, <u>listens</u>, <u>gardens</u>, <u>lessons</u>, <u>televisions</u>
ŋz   mornings, evenings, ceilings, things, rings, brings
lz   balls, girls, hills, hotels, meals, schools, smiles, walls, calls, pulls, <u>pupils</u>, <u>apples</u>, <u>examples</u>, <u>animals</u>, <u>pencils</u>, <u>bicycles</u>

Pronunciation of some words in this unit

Mr	mɪstə	James	dʒeɪmz
Mrs	mɪsɪz	**Wil**son	wɪlsn
Miss	mɪs	**break**fasts	brekfəsts
Ms	mɪz or məz	**stu**dents	stju:dnts
Jones	dʒəʊnz	rides	raɪdz
Smith	smɪθ	**bi**cycles	baɪsɪklz
Young	jʌŋ	**tele**phones	teləfəʊnz
loves	lʌvz	**wa**shes	wɒʃɪz
watches	wɒtʃɪz	**tea**ches	ti:tʃɪz
horses	hɔ:sɪz	**ma**tches	mætʃɪz
clothes	kləʊðz		

Ship or Sheep?

Teacher's notes on *Ship or Sheep?* are considerably shorter than for *Tree or Three?* As most units of *Ship or Sheep?* follow the same general plan it is possible to make suggested lesson procedures for all units (outlined below). Suggestions for further practice are not included as extensive practice material is already provided in the student's book. To avoid duplication of material, for information on student difficulties in each unit teachers are referred to the relevant pages under the section on *Tree or Three?*

Teacher's material for each unit

This is usually divided under the following headings:

Student difficulties

(See page 6 of this book).

Linking up with course work

In this section some specific suggestions are made for linking up the material in the unit with other course work. In some units the link is made with teaching a specific structure, for example, Unit 6 a: with practice of short answers using *are/aren't*; *can/can't*. In other units the link is more functional, for example, Unit 31 z with practice of formal introductions.

Word stress practice

This section has been included in answer to teachers' requests for more practice material on word stress patterns at this level. It generally contains words from the unit being taught, but occasionally words from other units are included. Often the material is presented in the form of a recognition test, but it is suggested that the stress patterns be practised first before the test.

SUGGESTED TEACHING PROCEDURES FOR WORD STRESS PRACTICE

i) Draw one of the stress patterns on the blackboard, making the dots larger and darker to represent stressed syllables and smaller and lighter to represent unstressed syllables. Tap out this pattern with a ruler or pencil and/or show the pattern by clapping. Students should join in.

ii) Students listen to and repeat the words with this stress pattern to the accompaniment of tapping or clapping. Whenever possible include other words of this stress pattern from the students' known vocabulary.

iii) Write the words on the blackboard and repeat step (ii) above.

iv) Students read the words from the blackboard.

v) Repeat steps (i)–(iv) above for the other stress pattern(s).

vi) Recognition Test. Erase all of this material from the blackboard except the stress pattern dots numbered A, B etc. as in the text of the test. Students write numbers 1–10 in their notebooks, then listen to each item of the test and write the letter to represent the correct pattern.

Pronunciation of some words in this unit

This section is included particularly for teachers whose mother tongue is not English, but native speakers may also find it useful to refer to.

Suggested lesson procedures

Note: Steps 2–4 are omitted in lessons where the minimal pairs are not yet introduced: p, t, k, s, m, l, i:. A slightly different approach has also been used in the lessons on the sounds ʒ and ə.

1 Diagram and notes

Make sure that students understand how the sound is made. Demonstrate where possible and model the sound.

Students practise the sound in isolation. Even with a large class it is possible to check every student's performance at this stage. The teacher will be free to give further individual help to those who need it during the group work later.

2 Minimal pairs

Check understanding of vocabulary. Where necessary illustrate by demonstration or putting the word in a sentence suitable to the class level.

Students listen and repeat the words, reading from the list first vertically then horizontally.

Example: **sound 1**   **sound 2**
            sheep   ship
            bean   bin
            seat   sit

Practise in this order:
a) sheep, bean, seat
b) ship, bin, sit
c) sheep/ship; bean/bin; seat/sit

The last stage in this practice (c) can be left till after step 3 below.

3 Recognition practice

The teacher reads words at random from the list of minimal pairs and students say if they heard sound 1 or sound 2.
Example: Teacher: bean
           Students: sound 2

           Teacher: ship
           Students: sound 1
Step (c) above can be practised here. Later, individual students can be asked to take the part of the teacher in the recognition practice.

4 Recognition test

Students tick the words they hear in the sentences read by the teacher or recorded on cassette. See page 165 of the Student's Book.

5 Word list

These are the unillustrated Practice lists. Students listen and repeat, reading the lists vertically. These are words the students will meet in the Dialogue. In the lessons on the sounds p and t this section has been omitted as the vocabulary has already been covered in the earlier practice lists.

6 Dialogue

This is a reading activity, but students may wish to listen and repeat sentences after the teacher first, depending on their reading ability.

7 Stress/intonation

Students listen and repeat.

8 Conversation/group work

In most lessons the final activity is a guided conversation or some other group work which is designed so that students practise both the sound and the stress/intonation learnt in the lesson. First check that the students know what to do by doing a few examples with the whole class listening.

While the students are involved in group work the teacher should be free to give further individual help to those who need it. During the group work time students can be asked to act the Dialogue in parts as well as the activity suggested in this section.

Unit 1 i: (sheep)

Student difficulties

See page 23.

Linking up with course work

Link with practice of
a) language used to choose items from a menu and make orders in a restaurant;
b) questions with 'would', for example: 'What would you like to . . . ?' 'Would you like . . . or . . . ?'

Word stress practice

●•   Edith, evening, sandwich, ice-cream, restaurant, menu, waiter, order, coffee
●•• vegetables, sandwiches, somebody, dialogue

Pronunciation of some words in this unit:

Edith	iːdɪθ	**ev**ening	iːvnɪŋ
Jean	dʒiːn	**res**taurant	restrɒ̃(t)
Peter	piːtə	**veg**etables	vedʒtəblz
menu	menjuː	**pea**ches	piːtʃɪz
waiter	weɪtə		

Unit 2 ɪ (ship)

Student difficulties

See page 25.

Linking up with course work

Link with practice of
a) numbers 20, 30, 40, etc.
b) conditional sentences using 'if'.

Word stress practice

See page 26 *Suggested procedures* for Exercise 3 Step 2.

Pronunciation of some words in this unit

interesting	ɪntrəstɪŋ	**thir**ty	θɜːtɪ
Indians	ɪndɪənz	**se**venty	sevntɪ
Lyn	lɪn	**bin**go	bɪŋgəʊ

Unit 3   e (pen)

Student difficulties

See page 41.

Linking up with course work

Link with practice of
a) 'wh' questions;
b) talking about holidays: 'How did you spend your holiday?' 'I went
    to ....';
c) offering food etc. at a social function, for example: Have some sugar (a
    biscuit)/Help yourself to sugar (biscuits).

Word stress practice

●••   holiday, everything, anything, interesting
●•••   everybody, Edinburgh, television, helicopter

Pronunciation of some words in this unit

Eddie	edɪ	**Ve**nice	venɪs
Ellen	elən	**Bel**gium	beldʒəm
Jenny	dʒenɪ	**Den**mark	denmɑːk
statements	steɪtmənts	Edinburgh	edɪnbʌrə

Unit 4   æ (man)

Student difficulties

See page 42.

Linking up with course work

Link up with practice in describing people to show which one is meant, for example:
'Look at that man.'
'Which one? The man with the black slacks?'
'No. That one with the camera.'

Pronunciation of some words in this unit

Bradley   brædlɪ   **Am**sterdam   æmstədæm
Allen   æ/lən   conversation   kɒnvəseɪ∫n
                            stressed   strest

Unit 5   ʌ (cup)

Student difficulties

See page 44.

Linking up with course work

Link with practice of:
a) *mustn't*/*must* (stressed);
b) comparisons using 'much ... than', for example, in comparing different types of cars:
   X is much better/cheaper/nicer/faster/stronger/bigger/less expensive/ more comfortable than Y;
c) asking the price of things using 'How much is this ... ?';
d) short answers using *does*/*doesn't*.

Word stress practice

Recognition test: A ●•• B •●•
1 company (A)   2 wonderful (A)   3 unhappy (B)   4 butterfly (A)
5 sunglasses (A)   6 sentences (A)   7 dialogue (A)   8 remember (B)
9 example (B)   10 comfortable (A)

Pronunciation of some words in this unit

London lʌndən   **com**fortable kʌmftəbl
dozen dʌzn   **on**ion ʌnɪən
tongue tʌŋ   **co**loured kʌləd
blood blʌd

Unit 6   ɑː (heart)

Student difficulties

See page 47.

Linking up with course work

Link with practice of:
a) short answers with *are/aren't*; *can/can't*;
b) telling the time using 'half past'.

Word stress practice

Recognition test: A ●••   B •●•
1 vegetables (A)   2 wonderful (A)   3 fantastic (B)   4 expensive (B)
5 comfortable (A)   6 company (A)   7 unhappy (B)   8 example (B)
9 remember (B)   10 photograph (A)

Pronunciation of some words in this unit

Margaret mɑːgrɪt   gui**tar** gɪtɑː
Barbara bɑːbrə   **mar**vellous mɑːvləs
Martha mɑːθə   **pho**tograph fəʊtəgrɑːf
Arnold ɑːnld   un**u**sual ʌnjuːʒʊəl
Charles tʃɑːlz

Unit 7   *Review*

Word stress recognition test

A ●•   B •●
1 review (B)   2 lovely (A)   3 uncle (A)   4 guitar (B)   5 perhaps (B)
6 cousin (A)   7 minutes (A)   8 yourself (B)   9 hello (B)   10 Mrs (A)

Unit 8 ɒ (clock)

Student difficulties

See page 51.

Linking up with course work

Link with practice of:
a) 'What's wrong?' 'I've got a headache, backache, etc.';
b) telling the time using 'What's the time?' and 'o'clock';
c) apologising using 'Sorry'.

Word stress practice

●•• horrible, popular, hospital, holiday, following
•●•• advertisement, binoculars, America, unusual

Pronunciation of some words in this unit

advertisement ədvɜːtɪsmənt   hospital hɒspɪtl
onwash ɒnwɒʃ   binoculars bɪnɒkjʊləz
restaurant restrɒ̃(t)   competition kɒmpətɪʃn

Unit 9 ɔː (ball)

Student difficulties

See page 52.

Linking up with course work

Link up with practice of:
a) the greeting 'Good morning';
b) telling the time using *quarter to/past*.

Word stress practice

Recognition test: A •● B● •
1 report (A) 2 repeat (A) 3 morning (B) 4 always (B) 5 arrive (A)
6 airport (B) 7 awful (B) 8 surprise (A) 9 football (B)
10 towards (A)

Pronunciation of some words in this unit

Audrey ɔ:drɪ   an**noun**cer ənaʊnsə
George dʒɔ:dʒ   **au**dience ɔ:dɪəns
Dawn dɔ:n   drawer drɔ:
Paul pɔ:l

Unit 10 ʊ (book)

Student difficulties

See page 70.

Linking up with course work

Link up with practice of:
a) greetings: 'Good morning/afternoon/evening';
b) question tags using *should/could/would*;
c) polite requests using *could* and *would*, for example: 'Could you open the door/shut the window/pass the sugar, please?'

Stress practice

●•   woman, bookshelf, bedroom, somewhere, didn't, couldn't, wouldn't, shouldn't
●•• cookery, living-room, didn't you, couldn't he, wouldn't we, shouldn't you

Pronunciation of some words in this unit

bedroom bedrʊm/bedru:m   **should**n't ʃʊdnt
couldn't kʊdnt   **would**n't wʊdnt

Unit 11 u: (boot)

Student difficulties

See page 72.

Linking up with course work

Link up with practice of:
a) the greeting 'Good afternoon';
b) questions beginning with *who* or *whose*;
c) short answers or question tags using *do* (Simple Present tense).

Word stress practice

●●•   nuisances, shoelaces, chewing gum, football boots, swimming pool
●••• supermarket, television, cookery books, newspaper stand

Pronunciation of some words in this unit

fruit juice   fruːt dʒuːs   **su**permarket   suːpəmɑːkɪt
ex**cuse** me   ɪkskjuːz miː

Unit 12   ɜː (girl)

Student difficulties

See page 56.

Linking up with course work

Link up with practice of short answers and question tags using *were/weren't*.

Word stress practice

●•   nurses, dirty, thirsty, German, Turkish, colonel, Herbert, Burton,
     Thursday (other days of the week except Saturday).

Pronunciation of some words in this unit

colonel   kɜːnl   **Tur**ner   tɜːnə
Burton   bɜːtn   **cur**tains   kɜːtnz
Herbert   hɜːbət   worst   wɜːst

Unit 13   ə (a camera)

Student difficulties

See page 16.

Linking up with course work

Link up with practice of use of weak forms in:
a) questions and statements with the following: *do, does, was, were, have, am, are, has, can*;
b) talking about the time: 'What's the time?' 'It's one o'clock/It's a quarter to six.'

Word stress practice

Recognition test: A •• ● B ● •• C • ●•
1 shoelaces (B) 2 important (C) 3 envelope (B) 4 afternoon (A)
5 cigarettes (A) 6 italics (C) 7 comfortable (B) 8 understand (A)
9 address book (C) 10 envelope (B)

Pronunciation of some words in this unit

Supermarket suːpəmɑːkɪt to**bac**conist's təbækənɪsts
comfortable kʌmftəbl

Unit 14 *Review*

Word stress recognition test

A • ● B ● •
1 perhaps (A) 2 polite (A) 3 open (B) 4 instead (A) 5 stupid (B)
6 foolish (B) 7 aloud (A) 8 spelling (B) 9 correct (A) 10 really (B)

Unit 15 eɪ (tail)

Student difficulties

See page 91.

Linking up with course work

Link up with practice of apologies beginning 'I'm afraid . . .', for example:
I'm afraid you've made a mistake/you'll have to wait/you're late. I'm afraid
I'm late/I've broken this plate/I've forgotten your name/I've lost your
newspaper/I don't know the date/I haven't any change.

Word stress practice

Recognition test: A ●• B •●
1 today (B) 2 mistake (B) 3 April (A) 4 afraid (B) 5 railway (A)
6 station (A) 7 surprise (B) 8 birthday (A) 9 away (B) 10 repeat (B)

Pronunciation of some words in this unit

porter pɔːtə   Grey greɪ
dangerous deɪndʒərəs   **sta**tion steɪʃn

Unit 16   aɪ (fine)

Student difficulties

See page 94.

Linking up with course work

Link up with practice of:
a) talking about likes and dislikes, for example: I like/don't like/don't mind ice-cream/white wine/fried rice/pies/pineapple/trifle;
b) offering things using 'Would you like . . . ?', for example: 'Would you like some ice-cream?';
c) *Goodbye/Goodnight.*

Word stress practice

Recognition test: A ●• B •●
1 typing (A) 2 never (A) 3 sometimes (A) 4 tonight (B)
5 typist (A) 6 goodbye (B) 7 behind (B) 8 never (A) 9 silence (A)
10 all right (B)

Pronunciation of some words in this unit

Mike maɪk   Miles maɪlz
Myra maɪərə   **li**brary laɪbrɪ
Violet vaɪələt   **ice** skating aɪs skeɪtɪŋ
Nigel naɪdʒl   ex**ci**ting ɪksaɪtɪŋ

Unit 17   ɔɪ (boy)

Student difficulties

See page 93.

Linking up with course work

Link up with practice in talking about what students enjoy, for example: 'I enjoy/don't enjoy (horseriding, football, walking, water skiing, drawing, sports, noisy parties).'

Word stress practice

●• garage, awful, boyfriend, motor, visit, madam,
•● perhaps, enjoy, destroyed, annoy, Rolls Royce.

Pronunciation of some words in this unit

Joyce   dʒɔɪs   annoying   ənɔɪɪŋ
awful   ɔ:fl

Unit 18   *Review*

Word stress recognition test

A ●•   B •●
1 paper (A)   2 enjoy (B)   3 perhaps (B)   4 birthday (A)   5 behind (B)
6 trying (A)   7 letter (A)   8 tonight (B)   9 beside (B)   10 railway (A)

Unit 19   aʊ (house)

Student difficulties

See page 78.

Linking up with course work

Link up with practice of:
a) formal introductions: 'How do you do?';
b) 'How are you?' 'How's your sister?' etc.;
c) questions beginning *How many/How much*.

Pronunciation of some words in this unit

lounge laʊndʒ   our aʊə   (weak form ɑː)
throw θrəʊ   ours aʊəz

Unit 20 əʊ (phone)

Student difficulties

See page 79.

Linking up with course work

Link up with practice of:
a) talking about future actions, for example: 'What are you going to do tomorrow?' 'I'm going to ....';
b) negative short answers: 'No, I don't/No, I won't.'

Word stress practice

●● sleeping, minutes, window, only, snowball, rhyming, crossword, answer, meaning, lonely, pillow, yellow
●● hello, ago, again

Pronunciation of some words in this unit

rhyme raɪm   Jones dʒəʊnz

Unit 21 *Review*

Word stress practice

●● Jones's, mountain, narrow, yellow, roses, growing, over
●● hotel, hello, ago, around

Unit 22 ɪə (beer)

Student difficulties

See page 67.

Linking up with course work

Link up with practice of:
a) 'Here you are', when giving something to someone;
b) toasts when drinking: 'Cheers! Here's to . . .'

Word stress practice

Recognition test: A ●● ● B ● ●●
1 cigarette (A)   2 sentences (B)   3 terrible (B)   4 disappear (A)
5 holiday (B)   6 typewriter (B)   7 understand (A)   8 atmosphere (B)
9 mountaineer (A)   10 Japanese (A)

Pronunciation of some words in this unit

bearded bɪədɪd   **Aus**tria ɒstrɪə
atmosphere ætməsfɪə   mountai**neer** maʊntɪnɪə

Unit 23   eə (chair)

Student difficulties

See page 67.

Linking up with course work

Link up with practice of questions beginning *Where*.

Word stress practice

● ●●   carefully, envelope, hairbrushes, everywhere, anywhere.

Pronunciation of some words in this unit

Claire kleə   pro**nounced** prənaʊnst
Mary meərɪ   **ev**erywhere evrɪweə

Unit 24 p (pen)

Student difficulties

See page 96.

Linking up with course work

Link up with practice of requests beginning *Please . . .*, *Help me to . . .*

Word stress practice

Recognition test: A •●   B ●•
1 passport (B)   2 surprise (A)   3 airport (B)   4 present (B)
5 repeat (A)   6 upstairs (A)   7 Paris (B)   8 pocket (B)   9 plastic (B)
10 perhaps (A)

Pronunciation of some words in this unit

piano pjænəʊ   **spid**er spaɪdə
Peter pi:tə   ex**pen**sive ɪkspensɪv

Unit 25 b (baby)

Student difficulties

See page 96.

Linking up with course work

Link up with practice of:
a) the greeting 'Happy Birthday';
b) sentences with *but*.

Word stress practice

Recognition test: A ●••   B •●•
1 remember (B)   2 policeman (B)   3 tomorrow (B)   4 beautiful (A)
5 butterfly (A)   6 important (B)   7 passenger (A)   8 terribly (A)
9 December (B)   10 example (B)

Pronunciation of some words in this unit

ex**am**ple ɪgzɑ:mpl   po**lice**man pəli:smən
postman pəʊstmən   **Bar**bara bɑ:brə
birthday bɜ:θdeɪ

Unit 26   t (tin)

Student difficulties

See page 74.

Linking up with course work

Link up with practice in:
a) asking and telling the time;
b) negative short answers.

Word stress practice

Recognition test: A ●●●   B ●●●
1 assistant (B)   2 opposite (A)   3 department (B)   4 gentleman (A)
5 lavatory (A)   6 telephone (A)   7 exactly (B)   8 quieter (A)
9 tomato (B)   ʹ10 agency (A)

Pronunciation of some words in this unit

restaurant	restrɒ̃(t)	photographer's fətɒgrəfəz
lavatory	lævətrɪ	cafeteria kæfɪtɪərɪə
basement	beɪsmənt	tomato təmɑːtəʊ

Unit 27   d (door)

Student difficulties

See page 76.

Linking up with course work

Link up with descriptions of actions in the past using:
a) the Simple Past tense;
b) the Past Perfect tense.

Word stress practice

Recognition test: A ●●   B ●●
1 forgot (A)   2 goodbye (A)   3 darling (B)   4 repaired (A)
5 answered (B)   6 children (B)   7 damaged (B)   8 hello (A)
9 today (A)   10 decide (A)

Pronunciation of some words in this unit

damaged   dæmɪdʒd   Donald   dɒnəld
Daisy   deɪzɪ   Dunston   dʌnstən
TV   tiː viː

Unit 28   k (key)

Student difficulties

See page 98.

Linking up with course work

Link up with practice of:
a) telling the time using the words *o'clock, quarter*;
b) third person singular of Simple Present tense of verbs ending with this
    sound, for example: *asks, makes, likes, looks, speaks, takes, walks, drinks,
    cooks, thinks.*

Word stress practice

Recognition test: A ●●●   B ●●●
1 electric (A)   2 coffee cup (B)   3 exciting (A)   4 collector (A)
5 exactly (A)   6 coke bottle (B)   7 expensive (A)   8 comfortable (B)
9 cuckoo clock (B)   10 excuse me (A)

Pronunciation of some words in this unit

collector   kəlektə   electric   ɪlektrɪk
cuckoo   kʊkuː   chocolate   tʃɒklət

Unit 29   g (girl)

Student difficulties

See page 98.

Linking up with course work

Link up with practice of requests beginning 'Could you give me . . .'.

Word stress practice

Recognition test: A ●●   B ●●
1 again (B)   2 guitar (B)   3 forget (B)   4 England (A)   5 August (A)
6 begin (B)   7 repeat (B)   8 garden (A)   9 about (B)   10 party (A)

Pronunciation of some words in this unit

August   ɔːgəst   **Ca**rol   kærl
Craig   kreɪg   for**get**   fəget

Unit 30   s (sun)

Student difficulties

See pages 10, 81, 100.

Linking up with course work

Link up with practice of:
a) suggestions beginning *Let's*;
b) the Simple Present tense of verbs taking the sound s in the third person
    singular, for example: *asks, breaks, cooks, counts, drinks, drops, eats, forgets,*
    gets, keeps, likes, looks, makes, puts, shuts, sits, sleeps, speaks, stops, takes,
    waits, walks, wants, works, writes.

Word stress practice

●●   outside, instead, hotel, upstairs
●●   headaches, seaside, suitcase, special, biscuits, basket
●●●   sensible, photographs, Saturday, interesting, stupidly
●●●   expensive, exciting

Pronunciation of some words in this unit

Alice   ælɪs   **spe**cial   speʃl
biscuits   bɪskɪts   ciga**rettes**   sɪgərets

Unit 31   z (zoo)

Student difficulties

See pages 13, 81, 100.

Linking up with course work

Link up with practice of:
a) formal introductions – 'This is Mrs X/Mr Y';
b) Simple Present tense of verbs taking the sound z in the third person singular.

Word stress practice

Recognition test: A ●•• B •●•
1 telegram (A)   2 surprises (B)   3 post office (A)   4 sentences (A)
5 expensive (B)   6 sun-glasses (A)   7 electric (B)   8 amazing (B)
9 jazz records (A)   10 surprising (B)

Pronunciation of some words in this unit

Jones dʒəʊnz	**cou**sins kʌznz
sur**pri**sing səpraɪzɪŋ	**Su**san suːzn
scissors sɪzəz	clothes kləʊðz

Unit 32   ʃ (shoe)

Student difficulties

See page 83.

Linking up with course work

Link up with practice of:
a) talking about nationality;
b) structures with *shall*; *should*; *she*.

Word stress practice

••●• conversation, intonation, demonstration, information, operation, electrician

●••• television, everybody, anybody, supermarket, helicopter

Pronunciation of some words in this unit

Marsh   mɑːʃ   demonstration   demənstreɪʃn
Shaw   ʃɔː   shrunk   ʃrʌŋk
ma**chine**   məʃiːn   **spe**cial   speʃl

Unit 33   ʒ (television)

Student difficulties

See page 84.

Linking up with course work

Link up with practice of:
a)   the reply 'It's a pleasure';
b)   descriptions of daily routine using the word *usually*.

Word stress practice

Recognition test: A ●••• B •●•• C ••●•
1 demonstration (C)   2 unusual (B)   3 variety (B)   4 helicopter (A)
5 America (B)   6 intonation (C)   7 television (A)
8 department store (B)   9 conversation (C)   10 advertisement (B)

Pronunciation of some words in this unit

Asia   eɪʒə   **trea**sure   treʒə
pleasure   pleʒə   **mea**suring   meʒərɪŋ

Unit 34   tʃ (cherry)

Student difficulties

See page 86.

Linking up with course work

Link up with practice of questions beginning *Which, How much*.

Word stress practice

Recognition test: A ●•   B •●
1 chicken (A) 2 mushrooms (A) 3 shallots (B) 4 machine (B)
5 chilli (A) 6 powder (A) 7 mixture (A) 8 shampoo (B)
9 contains (B) 10 salad (A)

Pronunciation of some words in this unit

Cheshire tʃeʃə   **shallots** ʃəlɒts
cheddar tʃedə   **mush**rooms mʌʃrʊmz
recipe resəpɪ

Unit 35 dʒ (jam)

Student difficulties

See page 88.

Linking up with course work

Link up with practice of the Present Perfect tense with *just*.

Word stress practice

●•• dangerous, manager, agency, passenger, orange juice, minister, difficult, recipe

Pronunciation of some words in this unit

injured ɪndʒəd   **dan**gerously deɪndʒərəslɪ
damaged dæmɪdʒd   **Chur**chill tʃɜːtʃɪl

Unit 36 f (fan)

Student difficulties

See page 28.

Linking up with course work

Link up with practice of conditional sentences using *if*.

Word stress practice

●••   photograph, comfortable, telephone, beautiful, Grandfather, difficult
•●•• photographer

Pronunciation of some words in this unit

photograph fəʊtəgrɑːf   information ɪnfəmeɪʃn
photographer fətɒgrəfə   comfortable kʌmftəbl

Unit 37   v (van)

Student difficulties

See page 29.

Linking up with course work

Link up with practice in asking and talking about past experiences using
'Have you ever . . . ?' 'No. I've never . . .'

Word stress practice

●••   villagers, photograph, somebody
•●•   arriving, November.

Pronunciation of some words in this unit

Vera   vɪərə   **F**ebruary februrɪ
Victor vɪktə   **vill**agers vɪlɪdʒəz

Unit 38   w (window)

Student difficulties

See page 31.

Linking up with course work

Link up with practice in:
a) asking questions beginning: *why, what, where, when, which*;
b) talking about the future using *will*;
c) conditional sentences with *would*;
d) offering things: 'Would you like a . . . ?'

Word stress practice

●●   railway, weather, squirrels, quiet, counted, quickly
●●●   sandwiches, everywhere, wonderful

Pronunciation of some words in this unit

Wednesday   wenzdɪ   **Vic**tor   vɪktə
Wendy   wendɪ   **squi**rrels   skwɪrlz
Gwen   gwen   **qui**et   kwaɪət

Unit 39   j (yellow)

Student difficulties

See page 90.

Linking up with course work

Link up with practice in:
a)   positive short answers beginning *Yes*;
b)   talking about the past using *used to*;
c)   interviewing someone by asking questions beginning *Do you/Are you/Have you/Can you* etc.

Word stress practice

Recognition test: A ●●●   B ●●●   C ●●●
1 sausages (B)   2 newspaper (B)   3 yesterday (B)   4 millionaire (A)
5 remember (C)   6 beautiful (B)   7 produces (C)   8 understand (A)
9 wonderful (B)   10 excuse me (C)

Pronunciation of some words in this unit

uni**ver**sity   juːnɪvɜːsətɪ   **tu**ba   tjuːbə
Hugh **Young**   hjuː jʌŋ   **Eu**rope   jɔːrəp
million**aire**   mɪlɪəneə

Unit 40   h (hat)

Student difficulties

See page 48.

Linking up with course work

Link up with practice in:
a) the greetings 'Hello' and 'How are you?';
b) questions beginning *who, whose, how*;
c) structures with *have/has* and *his/her/hers*;
d) exclamations beginning *How*.

Word stress practice

Recognition tests: A • ●   B ● •
1 hello (A)   2 behind (A)   3 husband (B)   4 injured (B)   5 perhaps (A)
6 express (A)   7 awful (B)   8 herself (A)   9 happened (B)
10 all right (A)

A ● • •   B • ● •
1 ambulance (A)   2 hospital (A)   3 horrible (A)   4 important (B)
5 terrible (A)   6 unhappy (B)   7 accident (A)   8 anything (A)
9 holiday (A)   10 example (B)

Pronunciation of some words in this unit

injured	ɪndʒəd	**Hel**en	helən
operation ·	ɒpəreɪʃn	**Hil**da	hɪldə
helicopter	helɪkɒptə	**Har**old	hærld

Unit 41   θ (thin)

Student difficulties

See page 19.

Linking up with course work

Link up with practice in:
a) saying 'Thank you';
b) structures with *anything/something/nothing/everything*;
c) expressing opinions, beginning *I think*.

Stress practice

Oh no! The Smiths' house is worth thirty thousand pounds.

Students listen to the following sentences and reply to each with this sentence, stressing the appropriate words:

1 The Smiths' house is worth thirty thousand dollars.
2 The Smiths' house is worth thirty million pounds.
3 The Smiths' house is worth twenty thousand pounds.
4 The Smiths' house isn't worth thirty thousand pounds.
5 The Smiths' car is worth thirty thousand pounds.
6 The Jones's house is worth thirty thousand pounds.

Pronunciation of some words in this unit

mathematician   mæθəmətɪʃn   Edith   iːdɪθ
Judith   dʒuːdɪθ   Ethel   eθl
theatre   θɪətə

Unit 42 ð (the feather)

Student difficulties

See page 21.

Linking up with course work

Link up with practice of:
a) *this/that/these/those/the other(s)*;
b) stating preferences, beginning 'I'd rather ... than ...';
c) making comparisons, for example: 'The first car is faster than the second car';
d) talking about family photographs, for example: 'This is my mother/father/brother/grandmother/grandfather.'

Word stress practice

Recognition test: A ● ●●   B ● ●●
1 assistant (A)   2 prettier (B)   3 comfortable (B)   4 Miss Brothers (A)
5 together (A)   6 anything (B)   7 expensive (A)   8 another (A)
9 uglier (B)   10 certainly (B)

Pronunciation of some words in this unit

madam   mædəm   comfortable   kʌmftəbl
certainly   sɜːtnlɪ

Unit 43   m (mouth)

Student difficulties

See page 35.

Linking up with course work

Link up with practice in:
a) making guesses using *must*, for example: He must be ill/He must have lost it;
b) talking about obligations: I must study, etc;
c) questions beginning *How many/How much.*

Word stress practice

Recognition test: A ●●●   B ●●●
1 interesting (A)   2 marmalade (A)   3 important (B)   4 example (B)
5 cinema (A)   6 grandmother (A)   7 policeman (B)   8 tomorrow (B)
9 remember (B)   10 family (A)

Pronunciation of some words in this unit

Mitcham   mɪtʃəm   **mar**malade   mɑ:məleɪd
Cambridge   keɪmbrɪdʒ   **mar**vellous   mɑ:vləs

Unit 44   n (nose)

Student difficulties

See page 36.

Linking up with course work

Link up with practice of:
a) greetings 'Good morning/afternoon/evening';
b) asking and talking about abilities: 'Can you swim/speak German?' etc.;
c) negative short answers using *No ... isn't/haven't/hasn't* etc.

Word stress practice

●●●   agency, avenue, certainly
●●●   apartment, forbidden, eleven, good morning
●●●●   inexpensive, operation
●●●●●   accommodation

Pronunciation of some words in this unit

apartment əpɑ:tmənt   **te**levision telɪvɪʒn
Mason meɪsn   **A**venue ævənju:
bingo bɪŋgəʊ

Unit 45   ŋ (ring)

Student difficulties

See page 38.

Linking up with course work

Link up with practice of:
a) greetings 'Good morning/Good evening';
b) continuous tenses with 'ing' verb endings;
c) asking and talking about preferences in sport and other leisure activities:
    'Do you like swimming/playing tennis/watching football/dancing?' etc.

Word stress practice

●● morning, singing, banging, standing, hanging, holding, shouting,
running, sleeping.

Pronunciation of some words in this unit

Pring prɪŋ   King kɪŋ
pink pɪŋk

Unit 46   l (letter)   Part 1

Student difficulties

See page 59.

Linking up with course work

Link up with practice of:
a) the greeting 'Hello';
b) requests with *please*;
c) telling the time using *o'clock*.

Word stress practice

Recognition test: A ●● B ●●
1 lettuce (A) 2 olives (A) 3 salad (A) 4 repeat (B) 5 melon (A)
6 jelly (A) 7 o'clock (B) 8 complain (B) 9 hello (B) 10 waitress (A)

Pronunciation of some words in this unit

olives ɒlɪvz Allen ælən
usually juːʒlɪ Lily lɪlɪ

Unit 47 l (ball) Part 2

Student difficulties

See page 59.

Linking up with course work

Link up with practice of:
a) asking and talking about the future using the Simple Future tense;
b) *myself/yourself/himself* etc.

Word stress practice

●●● beautiful, difficult, bicycle, gentleman, wonderful, sensible, horrible,
miserable, comfortable, hospital

Pronunciation of some words in this unit

sensible sensəbl   special speʃl
fault fɔːlt   miserable mɪzrəbl
comfortable kʌmftəbl

Unit 48 r (rain) Part 1

Student difficulties

See page 61.

Linking up with course work

Link up with practice of:
a) replies to 'How are you?': *Very well/All right*;
b) talking about colours. The following give practice in the sound l and r:
   red, green, grey, brown, orange, cream, yellow, blue, black, purple, lilac, pale green, pale blue etc.

Word stress practice

Recognition test: A ●••   B •●•   C •●••   D ••●•
1 sensible (A)   2 librarian (C)   3 secretary (A)   4 everywhere (A)
5 Australia (C)   6 interesting (A)   7 America (C)   8 electrician (D)
9 expensive (B)   10 photographer (C)

Pronunciation of some words in this unit

Randal rændl	**Ruth** ruːθ
Rita riːtə	**Lau**ra lɔːrə
Rosemary rəʊzmərɪ	**Ro**land rəʊlənd
Aus**tra**lia ɒstreɪlɪə	**Aus**tria ɒstrɪə
pho**tog**rapher fətɒgrəfə	**res**taurant restrɒ̃ or restrɒ̃t
library laɪbrɪ	elec**tri**cian elektrɪʃn
Europe jɔːrəp	li**bra**rian laɪbreərɪən

Unit 49   r (girl)   Part 2

Student difficulties

See pages 63 and 65.

Linking up with course work

Link up with practice of offering food:

Would you like	biscuits or some more	*eggs olives apples ice-cream omelette	onions apricots oranges oil apple pie	?

    *Also use words starting with a consonant to practice silent 'r' in *more* and *or*.

Word stress practice

Recognition test : A ●●   B ●●

1 upstairs (B)   2 quarter (A)   3 German (A)   4 weather (A)
5 depart (B)   6 New York (B)   7 forbid (B)   8 airport (A)
9 bookshop (A)

Pronunciation of some words in this unit

passengers	pæsndʒəz	e**mer**gency	ɪmɜːdʒənsɪ
for**bid**den	fəbɪdn	de**par**ture	dɪpɑːtʃə
wonderful	wʌndəfl	**fore**caster	fɔːkɑːstə

Diagnostic tests

Teacher's notes

The purpose of these tests is to determine students' weaknesses in pronunciation in order to find out which sounds need the most immediate attention for a particular class or language group. Each item in the reading passages ('Shopping List 1 and 2') tests one or two sounds.

Two alternative tests are included here, and the same result sheet can be used for either of these. The first of these tests is more suitable for near-beginners, who may if necessary be asked to repeat the items rather than read them.

Example:

SHOPPING LIST 2

1 three peaches (Get the Scotch peaches. These are cheaper.)

RESULT SHEET

1 i: (sheep)
  tʃ (cherry)

The Result Sheet shows that in item 1 the teacher must listen for the sounds i: and tʃ, and record the students' performance in these.

Administering the test

The test can be given to the whole class together if the students are of one mother tongue. Ask a number of students to read each test item and record an average of the results. If the class is of mixed nationality, it can be given to groups of students or to individuals. Students' performance can be tape-recorded, or students can be asked to repeat an item as many times as is necessary for the teacher to record the results.

The reasons for mispronunciation are many, and a large part of errors are spelling pronunciation. It is therefore advisable to check errors by saying the mispronounced words correctly and asking the student to repeat them.

Suggested symbols for grading

$\sqrt{}$ = no difficulty with this sound
× × = extreme difficulty
× = difficulty
× $\sqrt{}$ = minor difficulty.

The tests

Shopping list 1

1 some cheese (cheap cheese); some tea (Chinese tea)
2 fifty biscuits; four fish
3 ten eggs (big eggs)
4 jam; apples and oranges; a cabbage
5 ten tomatoes (large tomatoes)
6 five kilos of veal (very good veal)
7 some strong string (long string)
8 four forks (small forks); spoons; cups; small paper plates
9 some good sugar; milk; coffee; a cake
10 shoes for Mother (blue shoes); two kilos of fruit; rice (brown rice)
11 nuts; honey; one bun (a hot bun)
12 one lemon; nine brown onions; flowers for the house
13 some paper for Mother's letters (the cheaper paper); a pair of trousers for Father
14 a girl's shirt and a skirt; some cold drinks; bread (good bread)
15 eight cakes and paper plates; some sausages for supper
16 some yellow roses for your sister
17 white wine (sweet wine); some ice
18 beer for Bob (not the dear beer)
19 some shampoo for Mary's hair; some pears
20 tins of peas and beans (tins, please)
21 fish from the fish shop (English fish)
22 a toy for the boy (a little blue or yellow ball)
23 something for Mr Smith (it's his birthday on Thursday)
24 a television

Shopping list 2

1   three peaches (Get the Scotch peaches. These are cheaper.)
2   fifty biscuits (If they are cheap.)
3   ten eggs (Get big eggs.)
4   a jar of apple jam for Jack's sandwiches
5   tomatoes (Ask your aunt. Her garden isn't far from the market, and her tomatoes are marvellous.)
6   five servings of veal for this evening and some very good vodka
7   (Get a small bottle of vodka, because Uncle Oliver is bringing something strong to drink.)
8   a pork chop or some soup for Paul's supper; also four prawns for George
9   a good cookery book
10 choose two ripe grapefruit or buy some real fruit juice, perhaps orange or pear juice
11 a dozen hot buns for our unhappy uncle, perhaps honey buns
12 one pound nine ounces of brown flour
13 bacon (Remember that the bacon Father bought from Feather's was better than the bacon from the other grocer.)
14 a bird for David's thirteenth birthday
15 eight small cakes (Mrs May makes some tasty cakes.)
16 some yellow onions (Go to old Mr Jones in York Road.)
17 buy some sweet or dry white wine, and some ice
18 beer for Bob and Robert (Buy it from the pub near here.)
19 some pears (Compare the pears in the market with the pears in Mr Claire's.)
20 a dozen tins of New Zealand peas, or frozen peas
21 fresh English fish from the fish shop
22 a loin or joint for boiling; some olive oil; a leg of lamb
23 three unusual things for Arthur Smith:
24 a television; a measuring tape; some rouge

Result sheet

1 i: (sheep) ....
    tʃ (cherry) ....

2 ɪ (ship) ....
    f (fan) ....

3 e (pen) ....
    g (girl) ....

4 æ (man) ....
    dʒ (jam) ....

5 ɑ: (heart) ....
    t (tin) ....

6 v (van) ....

7 ɒ (clock) ....
    ŋ (ring) ....

8 ɔ: (ball) ....
    p (pen) ....

9 ʊ (book) ....
    k (key) ....

10 u: (boot) ....
     r (rain) ....

11 ʌ (cup) ....
     h (hat) ....

12 n (nose) ....
     aʊ (house) ....

13 ə (a camera) ....
     ð (the feather) ....

14 ɜ: (girl) ....
     d (door) ....

15 eɪ (tail) ....
     s (sun) ....

16 əʊ (phone) ....
     j (yellow) ....

17 aɪ (fine) ....
     w (window) ....

18 ɪə (beer) ....
     b (baby) ....

19 eə (chair) ....
     m (mouth) ....

20 z (zoo) ....

21 ʃ (shoe) ....

22 ɔɪ (boy) ....
     l (letter) ....

23 θ (thin) ....

24 ʒ (television) ....

List of likely errors

This is an index of common errors made by different language groups. The page references in bold type are to *Tree or Three?* Other page references are to *Ship or Sheep?*

Arabic speakers

Vowels

Meaning is carried by consonants in Arabic; all vowels need practice.

ɪ (ship)	confused with e (pen), **37**, *10*
æ (man)	confused with ʌ (cups) and ɑ: (heart) **41, 43**, *17, 20*
ə (a camera)	**10, 27, 55**, *42*
eɪ (tail)	confused with e (pen) or aɪ (fine) **102, 106**, *48, 56*
əʊ (phone)	confused with ɔ: (ball) or ɜ: (girl) **87, 86**, *63, 62*
ɔ: (ball)	too short or confused with əʊ (phone) **52, 87**, *27, 63*
u: (boot)	confused with ʊ (book) **77**, *35*
ɪə (bear)	pronounced as spelling **72**, *66*
eə (chair)	as spelling or confused with ɪ: (sheep) **72**, *69*

Consonants

Difficulty with groups of consonants especially at the beginning of a word.

p	sounds close to b **108**, *79*
r	strongly trilled **65**, *160*
	pronounced where normally silent **68, 70**, *53, 163*
w	pronounced v **24**, *125*
θ (thin)	**12**, *133* (but the sound exists in classical Arabic)
ð (feather)	**14**, *138* (but the sound exists in classical Arabic)
v	pronounced f or b **23**, *121, 122*
g	confused with k **112**, *95*
ʒ (television)	pronounced ʃ (shoe) or z **93**, *106*
ŋ (ring)	pronounced ŋg or ŋk **34**, *148*
tʃ (cherry)	may be pronounced ʃ (shoe) **95**, *108*
d	may be pronounced t in final position **81**, *86*

Intonation and stress

Arabs may sound abrupt, commanding.
Rising tune. **7, 29, 45**, *39* (and almost all intonation exercises)
Joining words. **89**, *69, 71, 105*

Chinese speakers

Vowels

ɪ (ship)	**18**, *6*
e	confused with æ (man) **39**, *13*
æ (man)	confused with ʌ (cup) or e (pen) **41, 39**, *17, 13*
ʌ (cup)	confused with ɑ: (heart) **44**, *21*
ʊ (book)	confused with u: (boot) **77**, *35*
u: (boot)	may be pronounced y (as in French *tu*) **77**, *34*
eɪ (tail)	pronounced e **102**, *48*

Final consonants may be dropped, especially after:

eɪ (tail)	**102**, *48*
əʊ (phone)	**87**, *61* and other diphthongs.

Consonants

Great difficulty with groups of consonants, especially finally, where one or more may be dropped.

l	confused with r **65**, *161*
z	sounds close to s, especially finally **6, 116**, *101*
dʒ	sounds close to tʃ (cherry) **97**, *112*
ʒ (television)	confused with ʃ (shoe) or z **93**, *106*
ʃ (shoe)	confused with s especially before i: or may sound close to h **91**, *103*
v	confused with w or f **24, 23**, *125, 121*
l	may be confused with n **60**, *154*
ŋ	confused with n **34**, *148*
ð (feather)	**14**, *138*
θ (thin)	**12**, *133*
b	pronounced p finally **108**, *74, 78*
d	pronounced t finally **81**, *87*
g	pronounced k finally **112**, *95*

Intonation

Falling tune. **4, 13, 47**, *5, 22, 33* (and almost all intonation exercises)
Expressing emotion. **75, 107, 113**, *22, 30, 49* etc.

Stress and rhythm

Sounds staccato.
Joining words. **89**, *69, 71, 105*

Czech and Polish speakers

Vowels

æ (man)	pronounced e **39**, *13*
æ (man)	confused with ʌ (cup) **41**, *17*
i: (sheep)	confused with ɪ (ship) **16**, **18**, *3, 6*
əʊ (phone)	pronounced ɒ **86**, *61*
ʊ (book)	confused with u: (boot) **77**, *35*
ə (a camera)	**10**, **27**, **55**, *42*

Consonants

w	pronounced v **24**, *125*
θ (thin)	**12**, *133*
ð (the feather)	**14**, *138*
ŋ (ring)	pronounced n, ŋk, or ŋg **34**, *148*
z	pronounced s in final position **6**, **116**, *101*
b	pronounced p in final position **108**, *74, 78*
d	pronounced t in final position **81**, *87*
g	pronounced k in final position **112**, *95*
v	pronounced f in final position **23**, *121*
dʒ (jam)	pronounced tʃ (cherry) in final position **97**, *112*
r	strongly trilled **65**, *160*
	pronounced where normally silent **68**, **70**, *53, 163*

Dutch speakers

Vowels

æ (man)	pronounced e **39**, *13*
ʌ (cup)	sounds close to ɜ: (girl) **41**, *16, 40*
əʊ (phone)	pronounced ɒ **86**, *61*
ɔɪ (boy)	second sound (ɪ) too long **104**, *53*
eɪ (tail)	second sound (ɪ) too long **102**, *47*

Consonants

w	sounds close to v or b **24**, *124*
z	pronounced s **6**, **116**, *100*
θ (thin)	**12**, *133*
ð (the feather)	**14**, *138*
g	pronounced k or x (loch) **112**, *94*
ʒ (television)	pronounced ʃ (shoe) **93**, *106*
ʃ (shoe)	pronounced s in final position **91**, *104*
dʒ (jam)	pronounced tʃ (cherry) in final position **97**, *113*
d	pronounced t in final position **81**, *87*
v	may be pronounced f **23**, *121*
b	pronounced p in final position **108**, *79*
ŋ (ring)	confused with n or nk in final position **34**, *148*

Finnish speakers

A tendency to pronounce words as they are spelt.

Vowels

æ (man)	pronounced e **39**, *13*
ɜ: (girl)	**58**, *37*
ə (a camera)	**10, 27, 55**, *42*
əʊ (phone)	**86**, *61*

Consonants

Final groups of consonants may cause difficulty.

w	pronounced v **24**, *125*
θ (thin)	**12**, *133*
ð (the feather)	**14**, *138*
g	confused with k **112**, *95*
b	confused with p especially finally **108**, *79*
f	confused with v especially finally **23**, *121*
z	pronounced s or ts **6, 116**, *101*
ʒ (television)	pronounced s or ts **93**, *106*
d	confused with t especially finally **81**, *87*
ʃ (shoe)	pronounced s or ts **91**, *103*
tʃ (cherry)	confused with ʃ (shoe) **95**, *109*
dʒ (jam)	pronounced tʃ (cherry) or j (yellow) **97**, *113*

French speakers

Vowels

ɪ (ship)	sounds close to i: (sheep) **18**, *7*
ʌ (cup)	confused with ɜ: (girl) **41**, *40*
əʊ (phone)	pronounced ɒ **86**, *61*
eɪ (tail)	pronounced e **102**, *48*
ʊ (book)	sounds close to u: (boot) **74, 77**, *31, 35*
ɔ: (ball)	may be confused with əʊ (phone) **52**, *27*
æ (man)	confused with ʌ (cup) **41**, *17*
ə (a camera)	**10, 27, 55**, *42*
ɔɪ (boy)	may be pronounced ɔ: (ball) **104**, *53*

Consonants

h	omitted or put in the wrong place **46**, *130*
θ (thin)	**12**, *133*
ð (feather)	**14**, *138*
r	too far back **65**, *160*
	pronounced where normally silent **68, 70**, *163*

n	may be nasalized in final position **31**, *145*
ŋ (ring)	may be nasalized in final position **34**, *148*
tʃ (cherry)	may be pronounced ʃ (shoe) **95**, *109*
t	has a different quality in French **79**, *82*

Intonation

Tends to be flat.
Falling tune. **4, 13, 16**, *5, 22, 30* (and almost all intonation exercises)
Questions. **7, 28, 45**, *5, 33, 126, 144,* etc.
Exclamations. **79, 80, 113**, *22, 132, 159*
Surprise. **79, 80**, *30, 49*

Stress

An area of great difficulty. All syllables tend to be stressed equally.
Word stress. **5, 10, 55**, *8, 15, 55, 81,* etc.
Sentence rhythm. **10, 27, 55**, *34, 44, 60* etc.

German speakers

Vowels

æ (man)	pronounced e **39**, *13*
əʊ (phone)	confused with ɔː (ball) **86**, *61*
ə (a camera)	**10, 27, 55**, *42*
ɔː (ball)	sounds close to ɒ **52**, *28*
ɜː (girl)	has a different quality in German **58**, *37*
aʊ (house)	has a different quality in German **84**, *57*

Consonants

w	pronounced v **24**, *125*
θ (thin)	**12**, *133*
ð (feather)	**14**, *138*
z	pronounced s in final position **6, 116**, *101*
d	pronounced t in final position **81**, *87*
g	pronounced k in final position **112**, *95*
b	pronounced p in final position **108**, *79*
v	pronounced f in final position **23**, *121*
ʒ (television)	may be pronounced ʃ (shoe) **93**, *106*
dʒ (jam)	may be pronounced tʃ (cherry) **97**, *113*
	or confused with j (yellow) *128*
tʃ (cherry)	sometimes pronounced ʃ (shoe) **95**, *109*
ŋ (ring)	may be confused with ŋg or ŋk **34**, *148*
r	too far back **65**, *160*
s	may be pronounced z at the beginning of a word **3, 6**, *101*
s + consonant	may be pronounced ʃ (shoe) at the beginning of a word *100*

Intonation and stress

Joining words. **89**, *69*, *71*, *105*

Greek speakers

Vowels

i: (sheep)	confused with ɪ (ship) **18**, *7*
æ (man)	confused with ɑ: (heart) **43**, *20*
ʌ (cup)	confused with ɑ: (heart) **44**, *21*
əʊ (phone)	pronounced ɒ **86**, *61*
ɔ: (ball)	confused with ɒ **52**, *28*
u: (boot)	confused with ʊ (book) **77**, *35*
eɪ (tail)	may be confused with aɪ (fine) or pronounced e **102**, *47*

Consonants

ʃ (shoe)	pronounced s **91**, *104*
ʒ (television)	pronounced z **93**, *106*
tʃ (cherry)	pronounced ts **95**, *108*
dʒ (jam)	pronounced dz **97**, *112*
w	may be pronounced gw or g **24**, *124*
h	pronounced x (loch) **46**, *130*
g	sounds close to j (yellow) in the middle of a word **112**, *94*
r	strongly trilled **65**, *160*
	pronounced where normally silent **68**, **70**, *163*
p	may sound close to b initially **108**, *74*, *79*
t	may sound close to d initially **79**, **81**, *82*, *87*
k	may sound close to g initially **112**, *90*, *95*
b	in final position may be confused with p **108**, *79*
d	in final position may be confused with t **81**, *87*
g	in final position may be confused with k **112**, *95*
v	in final position may be confused with f **23**, *121*
ð (feather)	in final position may be confused with θ **14**, *141*
z	in final position may be confused with s **6**, **116**, *101*
nd and nt	confused with d (sound d written 'nt' in Greek) **82**, *89*
mp	confused with b (sound b written 'mp' in Greek) **109**, *76*
ŋk and ŋg	confused with g **34**, *150*

Intonation

Falling tune. **4**, **13**, **16**, *5*, *22*, *30* (and almost all intonation exercises)
Joining words. **89**, *69*, *71*, *105*

Gujerati speakers

Vowels

æ (man)	confused with e **39**, *13*
ɔ: (ball)	confused with ɒ **52**, *28*
eɪ (tail)	pronounced e **102**, *48*
əʊ (phone)	pronounced ɒ **86**, *61*

Consonants

Difficulty with groups of consonants, expecially at the beginning of a word.

w	pronounced v or b **24**, *124*
θ (thin)	**12**, *133*
ð (feather)	**14**, *138*
t	pronounced with the tongue curled back **79**, *82*
d	pronounced with the tongue curled back **81**, *78*
z	sounds close to s especially finally **6**, *101*
ʒ (television)	may sound like ʃ (shoe) or j (yellow) **93**, *106*
ʃ (shoe)	may be confused with s **91**, *103*
l	found difficult at the end of a word **62**, *158*
r	pronounced where normally silent **68**, **70**, *163*

Intonation

Falling tune. **14**, **13**, **16**, *5*, *22*, *33* (and almost all intonation exercises)

Stress and Rhythm

Word stress. **5**, **10**, **55**, *15*, *55*, *82* (and all word stress exercises)

Hebrew speakers

Vowels

Meaning is carried by consonants in Hebrew. All vowels need practice.

æ (man)	confused with e or ʌ (cup) **39**, **41**, *13*, *17*
i: (sheep)	confused with ɪ (ship) **18**, *7*
ə (a camera)	pronounced close to e or as spelling **10**, **27**, **55**, *42*
ɜ: (girl)	pronounced close to e or as spelling **58**, *38*

Consonants

Difficulty with groups of consonants. Vowels inserted between consonants.

ð (feather)	**14**, *138*
θ (thin)	**12**, *133*
r	pronounced too far back or confused with w **65**, *160*
w	confused with r **24**, *124*
p	confused with f **22**, **108**, *74*, *116*
	(p and f represented by the same letter in Hebrew)
h	may be omitted **46**, *130*

Stress

Too even.
Word stress. **5, 10, 55,** *15, 55, 82* (and all word stress exercises)
Sentence rhythm. **10, 27, 55,** *34, 44, 60* (and all sentence rhythm exercises)

Hungarian speakers

Vowels

æ (man)	pronounced e **39,** *13*
ɪ (ship)	confused with iː (sheep) **18,** *7*
ɒ (clock)	confused with ɔː (ball) **49,** *28*
ɔː (ball)	confused with ʌ (cut) **41, 52,** *16, 27*
ʊ (book)	confused with uː (boot) **77,** *35*
eɪ (tail)	pronounced e **102,** *48*
əʊ (phone)	pronounced ɒ **86,** *61*
ə (a camera)	**10, 27, 55,** *42*

Consonants

w	pronounced v **24,** *125*
θ (thin)	**12,** *133*
ð (feather)	**14,** *138*
ŋ	pronounced ŋk or ŋg **34,** *149*
dʒ (jam)	pronounced dj (due) or tʃ (cherry) **97,** *113*

NOTE

letter c	may be pronounced ts
letter j	may be pronounced j (yellow)
letter s	may be pronounced ʃ (shoe)

Intonation

Sounds a little flat.
Exclamations. **79, 80, 113,** *22, 132, 159*
Surprise. **79, 80,** *30, 49*

Iranians (Farsi speakers)

Vowels

All vowels need practice.

ɪ (ship)	sounds close to iː (sheep) **18,** *7*
ɑː (heart)	sounds close to ɔː (ball) **43, 53,** *19, 27*
aɪ (fine)	sounds close to ɔɪ (boy) **105,** *50, 56*
əʊ (phone)	confused with ɔː (ball) **87,** *63*

ʊ (book)   confused with u: (boot) **77**, *35*
ə (a camera)   **10**, **27**, **55**, *42*
e   confused with ɪ (ship) and æ (man) **37**, **39**, *10*, *13*
æ (man)   confused with ʌ (cup) **41**, *17*
ɪə (beer)   **72**, *66*
eə (chair)   **72**, *69*

Consonants

Difficulty with groups of consonants especially at the beginning of a word.
w   confused with v **24**, *125*
θ (thin)   **12**, *133*
ð (feather)   **14**, *138*
s + consonant   difficult at the beginning of a word **3**, *100*
ŋ (ring)   pronounced ŋg **34**, *148*
r   pronounced where normally silent **68**, **70**, *163*

Stress

Word stress. **5**, **10**, **55**, *15*, *55*, *82* (and all word stress exercises)

Italian speakers

Vowels

ɪ (ship)   sounds close to i: (sheep) **18**, *7*
eɪ (tail)   sounds close to e or confused with aɪ (fine) **102**, **105**, *47*, *56*
əʊ (phone)   sounds close to ɒ **86**, *61*
ɔ: (ball)   confused with əʊ (phone) **52**, **87**, *27*, *63*
ɜ: (girl)   confused with ɔ: (ball) **58**, *38*
æ (man)   confused with ʌ (cup) **41**, *17*
ʌ (cup)   confused with ɑ: (heart) **44**, *21*
ʊ (book)   confused with u: (boot) **77**, *35*
ə (a camera)   **10**, **27**, **55**, *42*

Consonants

Difficulty with groups of consonants.
h   omitted or put in the wrong place **46**, *130*
θ (thin)   **12**, *133*
ð (feather)   **14**, *138*
z   confused with s **6**, **116**, *101*
s   pronounced z before m, l, n **4**, **89**, *98*, *100*
r   strongly trilled **65**, *160*
                  pronounced where normally silent **68**, **70**, *163*
ʒ (television)   confused with dʒ (jam) or ʃ (shoe) **93**, *106*
j (yellow)   confused with dʒ (jam) **100**, *128*
ŋ (ring)   **34**, *148*

Intonation and stress

Joining words: an extra vowel may be added at the end of a word. **89**, *69*, *71*, *105*

Japanese speakers

Vowels

Usually too short.

ɜ: (girl)	sounds close to ɑ: (heart) **58**, **43**, *37*
ə (a camera)	pronounced ɑ: (heart) or as spelling **10**, **27**, **55**, *42*
ɪ (ship)	sounds close to i: (sheep) **18**, *7*
æ (man)	confused with e (pen) **39**, *13*
ʌ (cup)	confused with æ (man) **41**, *17*
ʊ (book)	confused with u: (boot) **77**, *35*
eɪ (tail)	sounds close to e **102**, *48*
əʊ (phone)	sounds close to ɒ **49**, **86**, *24*, *61*
	or confused with ɔ: **87**, *63*
ɪə	**72**, *66*
eə	**72**, *69*

Consonants

l	sounds close to r **65**, *161*
f	confused with h **22**, **46**, *116*, *130*
θ (thin)	**12**, *133*
ð (feather)	**14**, *138*
v	sounds close to b **23**, *122*
w	found difficult in front of u: (boot) or ʊ (book) **24**, *124*
	when written *wh* may be pronounced f **25**, *126*
z	confused with s, especially finally **6**, *101*
	or pronounced dz or dʒ (jam)**6**, *100*
r	confused with l **65**, *161*
h	may sound close to ʃ (shoe) or f **46**, *130*
g	confused with k in final position **112**, *95*
ʒ (television)	pronounced dʒ (jam) or ʃ (shoe) **93**, *106*
n	confused with m or ŋ in final position **31**, *146*
j (yellow)	found difficult before ɪ (ship) or i: (sheep) **100**, *128*

Intonation

Falling tune. **4**, **13**, **16**, *5*, *22*, *33* (and almost all intonation exercises)

Stress and rhythm

Sounds staccato; an extra vowel may be added at the end of a word. Joining words. **89**, *69*, *71*, *105*

Kampucheans (Khmer speakers)

Vowels

ɪ (ship)	confused with i: (sheep) **18**, *7*
ʊ (book)	confused with u: (boot) **77**, *35*
ə (a camera)	pronounced as spelt **10**, **27**, **55**, *42*
æ (man)	confused with ʌ (cup) and e **39**, **41**, *13*, *17*
3: (girl)	sounds close to ɔ: (ball) **58**, *38*
eɪ (tail)	pronounced e **102**, *48*
əʊ (phone)	pronounced close to ɔ: (ball) **87**, *63*

Final consonants may be dropped after diphthongs.

Consonants

Great difficulty with groups of consonants, especially finally where one or more may be dropped.

z	may sound like s **6**, **116**, *101*
f	found difficult especially finally **22**, **116**
s	may sound close to h **3**, *97*
θ (thin)	**12**, *133*
ð (feather)	**14**, *138*
v	may be confused with w or sound close to b **23**, **24**, *125*, *122*
ʒ (television)	confused with dʒ (jam) **93**, *106*
ʃ (shoe)	confused with tʃ (cherry) **91**, **95**, *103*, *109*
dʒ (jam)	may be pronounced tʃ (cherry) in final position **97**, *112*
j (yellow)	may sound like dʒ (jam) **100**, *127*
k	may sound like t in final position **112**, *90*
l	confused with r after k or g **65**, *161*

Intonation

Falling tune. **4**, **13**, **16**, *5*, *22*, *33* (and all intonation exercises)
Expressing emotion. **79**, **80**, **113**, *22*, *30*, *49*, *132*, *159*

Stress and rhythm

Sound staccato.
Joining words. **89**, *69*, *71*, *105*

Portuguese speakers

Vowels

ɪ (ship)	sounds close to i: (sheep) **18**, *7*
æ (man)	confused with e **39**, *13*
ɑ: (heart)	pronounced 3: (girl) before m or n **43**, *19*
	or confused with æ (man) **43**, *20*

ʊ (book)   confused with u: (boot) **77**, *35*
ɔ: (ball)   confused with ɒ **52**, *28*
ə (a camera)   **10**, **27**, **55**, *42*
əʊ (phone)   sounds close to ɒ or ɔ: (ball) **86**, *61*
eɪ (tail)   pronounced e **102**, *48*

Consonants

Difficulty with groups of consonants; final consonants dropped or not pronounced clearly.

r   too far back, may sound close to h **65**, *160*
h   sometimes omitted **46**, *130*
θ (thin)   **12**, *133*
ð (feather)   **14**, *138*
b   may sound close to v **108**, *122*
tʃ (cherry)   pronounced ʃ (shoe) **95**, *108*
dʒ (jam)   pronounced ʒ (television) **97**, *112*
j (yellow)   sometimes omitted **100**, *127*
z   confused with s and ʒ (television) **6**, *101*
n   in final position may be nasalized or confused with m **31**, *146*
r   pronounced where normally silent **68**, **70**, *163*
s + consonant   found difficult at the beginning of a word **3**, *100*

Punjabi speakers

Vowels

æ (man)   confused with e **39**, *13*
ɔ: (ball)   **52**, *27*
ə (a camera)   sometimes confused with ʌ (cup) or as spelling **10**, **27**, **55**, *42*
əʊ (phone)   pronounced ɒ **86**, *61*
eɪ (tail)   pronounced e **102**, *48*

Consonants

Difficulty with groups of consonants especially at the beginning of a word.

v   confused with w **24**, *125*
θ (thing)   pronounced close to t **12**, *133*
ð (feather)   pronounced close to d **14**, *138*
p   may sound like b **108**, *79*
t   pronounced with the tongue curled back **79**, *82*
d   pronounced with the tongue curled back **81**, *86*
r   strongly trilled **65**, *160*
                      pronounced where normally silent **68**, **70**, *163*
ŋ   may be pronounced ŋg **34**, *148*

Intonation

Falling tune. **4**, **13**, **16**, *5*, *22*, *33* (and almost all intonation exercises)

Stress and rhythm

Word stress. **5**, **10**, **55**, *15*, *55*, *82* (and all word stress exercises)

Russian speakers

Vowels

æ (man)	pronounced e **39**, *13*
ɪ (ship)	confused with iː (sheep) **18**, *7*
ɜː (girl)	as spelling **58**, *37*
ə (a camera)	as spelling **10**, **27**, **55**, *42*
əʊ (phone)	pronounced ɒ **86**, *61*
eɪ (tail)	pronounced e **102**, *48*
ɒ	confused with ɔː (ball) **52**, *28*
ʊ (book)	confused with uː (boot) **77**, *35*

Consonants

θ (thin)	**12**, *133*
ð (feather)	**14**, *138*
w	pronounced v **24**, *125*
r	strongly trilled **65**, *160*
ŋ	pronounced n, ŋk or ŋg **34**, *148*
z	pronounced s in final position **6**, **116**, *101*
b	pronounced p in final position **108**, *79*
d	pronounced t in final position **81**, *87*
g	pronounced k in final position **112**, *95*
v	pronounced f in final position **23**, *121*
h	pronounced x (loch) **46**, *130*
p	may sound like b at the beginning of a word **108**, *74*, *79*

NOTE

Because of the Cyrillic alphabet:
letter B	may be pronounced v
letter C	may be pronounced s
letter P	may be pronounced r
letter H	may be pronounced n
letter d	may be pronounced g

Speakers of Swedish, Norwegian, Danish

Vowels

ɪ (ship)	sounds close to iː (sheep) **18**, *7*
əʊ (phone)	pronounced ɒ **86**, *61*
eɪ (tail)	final sound ɪ too long **102**, *47*
aɪ (fine)	final sound ɪ too long **105**, *50*
ɔɪ (boy)	final sound ɪ too long **104**, *53*

Consonants

θ (thin)	**12**, *133*
ð (feather)	**14**, *138*
w	often pronounced v **24**, *125*
dʒ (jam)	confused with j (yellow) or pronounced dj (due) by Danes **97**, **100**, *112*
z	may be pronounced s **6**, **116**, *100*
ʒ	sounds close to ʃ (shoe) **93**, *106*
tʃ (cherry)	confused with ʃ (shoe) or pronounced tj (tube) by Danes **95**, *109*

Intonation

Statements may sound like questions; sentences may sound incomplete. Falling tune. **4**, **13**, **16**, *5*, *22*, *33* (and almost all intonation exercises)

Serbo-Croat speakers

Vowels

ɪ (ship)	confused with iː (sheep) **18**, *7*
æ (man)	pronounced e **39**, *13*
	or confused with ʌ (cup) **41**, *17*
ɜː (girl)	confused with ɔː (ball) or as spelling **58**, *37*
ə (a camera)	as spelling **10**, **27**, **55**, *42*
əʊ (phone)	pronounced ɒ **86**, *61*
ʌ (cup)	confused with ɑː (heart) **44**, *21*
ʊ (book)	confused with uː (boot) **77**, *35*
ɪə (beer)	confused with iː (sheep) **72**, *67*
eə (chair)	confused with e **72**, *69*

Consonants

w	pronounced v **24**, *125*
θ (thin)	**12**, *133*
ð (feather)	**14**, *138*
ŋ (ring)	pronounced ŋg or ŋk **148**, *34*
r	strongly trilled **65**, *160*
p	may sound close to b **108**, *79*

z	pronounced s in final position **6**, **116**, *101*
b	pronounced p in final position **108**, *79*
d	pronounced t in final position **81**, *87*
g	pronounced k in final position **112**, *95*
v	pronounced f in final position **23**, *121*

NOTE
Because of the Cyrillic alphabet:

letter B	may be pronounced v
letter C	may be pronounced s
letter P	may be pronounced r
letter H	may be pronounced n
letter d	may be pronounced g

Spanish speakers

A strong tendency to pronounce words as they are spelt.

Vowels

ɪ (ship)	confused with i: (sheep) **18**, *7*
æ (man)	confused with ʌ (cup) **41**, *17*
ə (a camera)	pronounced as spelling **10**, **27**, **55**, *42*
ɜ: (girl)	pronounced as spelling **58**, *37*
ɔ: (ball)	confused with əʊ (phone) **87**, *63*
	or with ɒ **52**, *28*
əʊ (phone)	pronounced ɒ **86**, *61*
ʊ (book)	confused with u: (boot) **77**, *35*
eɪ (tail)	pronounced e **102**, *48*
ɪə (bear)	pronounced as spelling **72**, *66*
eə (chair)	pronounced as spelling **72**, *69*

Consonants

Difficulty with groups of consonants. Final consonants dropped or not pronounced clearly. Sometimes t is substituted for other final consonants.

v	pronounced b at the beginning of a word **23**, *122*
h	pronounced x (loch) **46**, *130*
j (yellow)	confused with dʒ (jam) **100**, *127*
z	pronounced s **6**, **116**, *101*
w	found difficult in front of u: (boot) or ʊ (book): may be pronounced b or gw **24**, *124*
d	sounds close to ð (feather) in the middle of a word **81**, *139*
ʃ (shoe)	pronounced tʃ (cherry) or s **91**, **95**, *103*, *109*
m	confused with n in final position **30**, *143*, *146*
ŋ (ring)	confused with n **34**, *148*
r	strongly trilled **65**, *160*
	pronounced where normally silent **68**, **70**, *163*
b	sounds close to v in the middle of a word **108**, *78*, *122*
s + consonant	difficult at the beginning of a word **3**, *100*

Intonation

Sounds a little flat.
Exclamations. **79, 80, 113**, *22*, *132*, *159*
Surprise. **79, 80**, *30*, *49*

Turkish speakers

A strong tendency to pronounce words as they are spelt.

Vowels

æ (man)	confused with e **39**, *13*
ʌ (cup)	confused with æ (man)**41**, *17*
ɑː (heart)	close to ʌ (cup) **43**, *21*
ʊ (book)	pronounced u: (boot) **77**, *35*
eɪ (tail)	close to e **102**, *48*
əʊ (phone)	pronounced ɒ or ɔ: (ball) **86**, *61*
ɪə (beer)	pronounced as spelling **72**, *66*
eə (chair)	pronounced as spelling **72**, *69*

Consonants

Difficulty with groups of consonants, especially at the beginning of a word.

w	pronounced v **24**, *125*
θ (thin)	**12**, *133*
ð (feather)	**14**, *138*
ŋ (ring)	pronounced ŋg or ŋk **34**, *148*
r	strongly trilled **65**, *160*
	or pronounced where normally silent **68, 70**, *163*
z	pronounced s in final prositon **6, 116**, *101*
b	pronounced p in final position **108**, *79*
d	pronounced t in final position **81**, *87*
g	pronounced k in final position **112**, *95*
v	pronounced f in final position **23**, *121*

Thai and Lao speakers

Vowels

May be nasalized after h, m or n.

ʊ (book)	confused with u: (boot) **77**, *35*
ɑː (heart)	confused with ʌ (cup) **43**, *21*
æ (man)	confused with e or ʌ (cup) **39, 41**,*13, 17*

Final consonants may be dropped especially after diphthongs.

eɪ (tail)	**102**, *48*
əʊ (phone)	**86**, *62*

Consonants

Great difficulty with groups of consonants, especially finally where one or more may be dropped.

l	confused with r **65**, *161*
	or may be pronounced n finally **60**, *154*
θ (thin)	**12**, *133*
ð (feather)	**14**, *138*
v	confused with w **24**, *125*
	or pronounced b in the middle of a word **23**, *122*
z	may be pronounced s **6**, **116**, *101*
ʒ (television)	confused with ʃ (shoe) or z **93**, *106*
dʒ (jam)	pronounced tʃ (cherry) **97**, *113*
g	may be pronounced k **112**, *95*

Intonation

All intonation exercises will be useful.

Stress

Sounds staccato.
Joining words. **89**, *69*, *71*, *105*

Urdu speakers

Vowels

May be nasalized.

ʌ (cup)	confused with ə (a camera) **41**, **10**, *16*, *42*
æ (man)	pronounced e **39**, *13*
ɜ: (girl)	pronounced as spelling **58**, *37*
ɪə (beer)	pronounced as spelling **72**, *66*
eə (chair)	pronounced as spelling **72**, *69*
eɪ (tail)	pronounced e **102**, *48*
əʊ (phone)	pronounced ɒ **86**, *61*

Consonants

Difficulty with groups of consonants.

w	confused with v **24**, *125*
θ (thin)	**12**, *133*
ð (feather)	**14**, *138*
r	strongly trilled **65**, *160*
	pronounced where normally silent **68**, **70**, *163*
t	pronounced with the tongue curled back or may sound like d
	at the beginning of a word **79**, **81**, *82*, *87*
d	pronounced with the tongue curled back **81**, *86*
p	may sound like b at the beginning of a word **108**, *79*
k	may sound like g at the beginning of a word **112**, *95*

Intonation

Falling tune. **4**, **13**, **16**, *5*, *22*, *33* (and almost all intonation exercises)

Stress

Word stress. **5**, **10**, **55**, *8*, *15*, *55* (and all word stress exercises)

Vietnamese speakers

Vowels

ɪ (ship)	confused with iː (sheep) **18**, *7*
æ (man)	confused with ʌ (cup) or e **39**, **41**, *13*, *17*
ʊ (book)	confused with uː (boot) **77**, *35*
ɒ	confused with ɔː (ball) **52**, *28*
ɜː (girl)	may sound close to ɔː (ball) **58**, *38*

Final consonants may be dropped, especially after diphthongs:

eɪ (tail)	**102**, *48*
əʊ (phone)	**86**, *62*

Consonants

Great difficulty with groups of consonants, especially finally where one or more may be dropped.

θ (thin)	**12**, *133*
ð (feather)	**14**, *138*
z	pronounced s in final position **6**, **116**, *101*
s	confused with t in final position **3**, **79**, *98*
f	confused with p in final position **22**, *117*
b	confused with p in final position **108**, *79*
d	pronounced t in final position **81**, *87*
l	confused with n finally **60**, *154*
r	may be pronounced z **65**, *160*
dʒ (jam)	pronounced ʒ (television) **97**, *112*
tʃ (cherry)	may be confused with t or ʃ (shoe) especially in final position **95**, *108*
ʃ (shoe)	may be confused with s or t **91**, *103*

Intonation

All intonation exercises will be useful.

Stress and rhythm

Sounds staccato.
Joining words. **89**, *69*, *71*, *105*